# UNMISPLACED GLORY

# UNMISPLACED GLORY

Ian Kimotho

EXCELLER BOOKS®
A GLOBAL PRESS

**Unmisplaced Glory**



Cover by Exceller Books using resources from Pixabay.com


ISBN: 978-93-48892-18-8

First published in India in 2025 by Exceller Books,
An imprint of GE Group

Address: G1, Dream Apartment, Degree College Road, Belgharia,
Kolkata, 700056, India
www.excellerbooks.com

EXCELLER BOOKS®
A GLOBAL PRESS

## Acknowledgement

I am grateful to acknowledge everyone who contributed to this work, directly or indirectly. First and foremost, I would like to thank God, who saw me reach this point long before it actually happened. I extend heartfelt thanks to my mother, who supported me through thick and thin to ensure I completed college. I am also grateful to Dove International Wellness Centre for helping me restore my sanity—you truly did a remarkable job.

To my aunt, Nyawira Charity, who always checks in on me, please receive my sincere gratitude. And to Madam Cate from Silwan, who believed in me and encouraged me throughout this journey, I truly appreciate you.

# Table of Contents

# Chapter | 1

There were some echoing gunshots. Whoever the victim was must have received a really huge blow. Alfonso first headed into his home, and the first sight that caught his eyes was inconceivable. He gasped for air; it was the worst debilitation he had ever encountered. On the floor, blood was all over, with his family's bodies lying lifeless. He tore his shirt and started pacing. He stared in disbelief as confusion befell him. "This can't be happening..." he thought to himself. To make matters worse, his dad had promised him a surprise that day. The blood made him fidget.

"Mommy... Daddy...," he was shocked that even his sister was one of them. "Please say a word, sister," he pleaded. Bitterness like he had never experienced overwhelmed him, and he yearned helplessly. "This must be the saddest day of my life." Feelings of desolation engulfed him as he contemplated the incident. The immediate neighbors streamed in to witness what was going on.

Tony was also present. "Can you accept such an act to go unreciprocated?" he asked Alfonso.

"No! Never!" Alfonso replied in an affirmative tone.

Feelings of rage consumed the young adult. He couldn't control his emotions. He looked forward to avenging what he was seeing in the most cynical way. By then, witnesses had begun to multiply.

He went and took a knife. Just as he came out of the kitchen, a man on the TV (there was a rerun of his favorite program) made a loud citation: "Well, I know you did not foresee this happening; just get prepared." Immediately, the people panicked (they couldn't connect the words with the scene in the living room). One of the witnesses excused herself to go and calm her anxiety, and Alfonso immediately followed her. Just as she turned to see who was behind her, Alfonso gave her a blow, sending her to the wall. He then squeezed her mouth with his hand so she couldn't make any noise and slit her throat into two halves, blood spilling all over the floor. "Huh! I can now breathe," he muttered.

He went back to the sitting room and called Tony. "These are the same people who killed my family and are pretending to be pitiful. Here is the deal: you take a knife, and we slaughter them."

"You have a point. If that will make you feel good, I am ready," Tony agreed. He went to the kitchen, took a knife, went to the sitting room door, and closed it. The witnesses grew uneasy upon seeing this act. One of them suspected that something fishy was going on. He ran fast toward the door and tried to escape, but Tony engaged him. The others, not understanding what was happening, tried to hide and scattered all over. Tony overpowered him and stabbed him in the stomach. But before he could move, he felt a seat hit his back—one of the witnesses had gathered courage. That's when Alfonso showed up, stabbing him in the chest. He cried out loudly before falling to the ground.

"So, you two should now be saying your last prayers."

Immense shock befell the two remaining witnesses. They had pressed themselves into one corner and were wailing bitterly. "At least don't kill us," they pleaded.

"Do you know the pain I am experiencing? You too will partake of it," Alfonso declared. He grabbed one and held him from behind. "Don't you like the experience?" They were juniors and were terrified to their wits. "Now I can avenge!" He pushed the knife through his abdomen. The victim fell to the floor with a bang. Tony went for the last one, who was trembling immensely. He lifted him up and urged Alfonso to strike for maximum pain. "Schunk!!" He pushed the dagger into his back, rolled it vigorously, removed it, licked it, and sighed, "Yeah, sweet revenge...!"

"Let me open the door for some fresh air, at least." No sooner had Alfonso opened the door than a running man entered the house. "Hey!!!!! Hey!!!!! You have to hide me; a police officer is chasing after me. I know you are experiencing something tragic from the look of things, but I'll explain later."

"Okay, you stay here, but know that there has just been a massacre here."

"No worries," he replied. They took him to the second bedroom as a police officer could be seen from the window approaching the house.

"Who are you, and where have you hidden him?" The officer hardened his face and was about to remove his handcuffs when he realized it was Alfonso.

"Alfonso!"

"Yes, Uncle."

Malcolm's eyes identified the three bodies. His strength depleted as he sat on the floor. "Now my brother is dead! And I had foreseen this happening with the high crime rate in this area. Now we have lost him!" Malcolm lamented.

They spent a few minutes with Alfonso trying to explain the chronology of events, from how he discovered the scene to how he became infuriated and brought down the four witnesses.

Some time elapsed with Mr. Malcolm still in shock. "Hey, Alfonso, you need to go to each of the neighbors and tell them that their kin have died, seeing that their relatives came to witness the murders and also perished. It could elicit doubts."

"Hurry," he urged. Malcolm called an ambulance, and all the bodies were taken to the morgue. Alfonso started an endeavor to convince the neighbors after changing his shirt.

There were three neighbors he could recognize, and he headed to the first one. "Hi."

"Oh, Alfonso, did the gunshots come from your home?" The neighbor was doing her laundry. "Are you alright?"

"Yes, we are alright, but we have some bad news."

"Bad news? Oh no, don't tell me your family was involved..."

"My family? No, it's your brother."

"My brother? Is he alright?"

"There was an armed robber hiding inside the house when your brother came to witness, and he eventually killed him. In fact, I escaped narrowly by hiding in the bathroom at his disguise..."

Her hands began trembling as she burst into wailing. Her lips trembled as she fell to the ground, her strength depleted. "I am sorry, but we have to go." Alfonso and Tony started leaving, comforting her that it would be alright.

They did the same for the other two and then returned home. They engaged the boy who had come running and offered to take him to his home. Upon arriving, Malcolm told them that he had informed other relatives and that they were on their way.

Later that evening, nearly all of Alfonso's father's and mother's siblings had arrived for the mourning. They sang solemn songs, and many engaged Alfonso in comforting words. Later, some left while others remained.

Burial preparations were underway as the bereaved planned the budget for the whole event, including the attires to be worn, the purchase of the casket, and the food to be taken during the ceremony.

"I can't believe that my family is gone," he was so stressed and wondered what would become of him.

"You look stressed, what's up?" one of her cousins inquired.

"I don't want to be alone..."

"Don't worry, I am here for you, and you have us—your cousins—okay?" She hugged him.

The second day arrived. That day, his aunt seemed enthusiastic as she approached him and promised that her son would come to keep him company.

"I know we can't replace Fredric and Susan, but we'll try our best... okay?"

When she mentioned them, Alfonso seemed as if he was about to shed some tears, but his aunt was alert enough and gave him a big hug.

Finally, it was Friday, and the burial commenced. They all looked somber as Alfonso contemplated their demise. They took breakfast and dived into the business of the day.

During the ceremony, Alfonso seemed overwhelmed with emotions, constantly wiping his tears. His closest cousin was unable to bear it and vanished from the compound in tears... It was such a despairing occasion. He only interred the bodies on Malcolm's assurance.

"I promise you, we shall get our revenge," he said, giving him a fist bump. That was the only thing that gave them some strength.

The day ended, and the mourners retreated to their homes—except Kingsley.

"Hey, cousin, you need to accompany me to pick my belongings."

"You can do that..."

"Oh no, you are still weak. It's okay..."

They cooked supper together in an attempt by Kingsley to calm Alfonso. Later, they slept. That was a day Alfonso would never forget.

Early the following day, Alfonso woke up first and began preparing breakfast, but when he went to check his phone, he caught a glimpse of his dad's portrait. The good memories they had together ran through his mind. A sharp sense of sorrow surfaced.

"Why did you leave me…" His voice broke. "Why!!!!!!!"

He took the portrait, sat on the floor, and stared straight at it.

"Whoever killed you will realize my full wrath, I promise you," he muttered. He held the photo to his chest and lay on the floor with it.

Kingsley woke up and immediately saw what was happening.

"Now, how do I handle such a situation? Do I call Mom?" he wondered.

He braced himself.

"Cousin, it's all right. Hand me the photo."

"But why?"

"Don't worry. Don't worry."

With a heavy heart, he handed over the photo.

"I'll take over making breakfast."

"Hey Tony, what are you doing?"

"Nothing, just chilling."

"Remember how we massacred those hypocrites? They thought they could just walk away like that."

Kingsley overheard their conversation. He approached them with a blank face.

"Massacre! People? I'm leaving here," he declared.

"What!! So what's the problem?"

"Not only have you killed, but you are cruel and insensitive!"

Immediately, he called his mom.

"Mom, imagine Alfonso was insensitively talking about murdering people with his friend…"

"Alfonso!!" She seemed as if she wanted to refute the claims.

"How sure are you that he's not talking about something else?"

"Mom, I heard it all."

"Let me call him and confirm…"

She called Alfonso, but he denied the claims.

"Yes, continue being a good boy."

"Okay, Auntie."

"Kingsley, he told me that he never said anything like that."

"Mom, you've just been fooled, I'm telling you."

The call ended.

"I must report you to the police. You can act innocent, but you won't go unpunished!"

"Ah! Do whatever you wish."

Kingsley banged the door and headed to the Kikuyu police station.

"Hi Tony," he called him for the second time.

"Hey, please, you need to make your way to our home," he said, breathing heavily.

"What is it?? What has transpired?"

"I must find a place to hide," he said nervously.

"Hide? Why?"

"Kingsley has headed to the police after eavesdropping on our last call."

Tony's face dimmed.

"That is so risky… Okay, give me about twenty minutes."

Alfonso opened the gate.

"Hurry!! Come…" He locked the gate behind them as he followed Tony.

They went to Kinoo and arrived at a compound with a black gate. They knocked.

"At least here, we'll be safe for the next few days..."

Something weird happened immediately—Morris opened the gate, but his face froze. Agitated, he banged it shut and retreated inside after seeing them.

Tony was confused and called him.

"Morris! Morris!"

Morris angrily shouted at him to never call his name again and never come there.

"Tony, are you certain you have not done anything wrong?"

"Nothing that I know of."

"Morris, what's wrong? It's me, your friend!"

They tried calling him again, but there was no answer.

"What could be wrong?" Alfonso asked Tony.

"So, what do we do?" Tony asked.

They had started walking back when two gentlemen called them.

"Hey, who are you, and why has Morris dismissed you?"

"Oh, we had come seeking a place to stay, but he told us that he never wanted to see us again."

"We are his friends."

"Why did you want to stay?"

"Oh sir, there were general renovations at our house, and we needed a place to stay, at least for a day or two."

"I have been friends with your son, and I have never seen him behave this way," one of the gentlemen asserted to the other.

"You guys mind coming to my home?"

"Sir, that would be very thoughtful of you, and we'd appreciate it."

So he bade goodbye to the other man as they left for the other's house.

"Guys, have you eaten Morris' pie?" he joked.

It took about ten minutes, and they finally arrived. "Have you guys taken breakfast?"

"Actually, we wouldn't mind."

"Sir, how do you live in this big house alone?" They were puzzled by the size of the house, yet he was alone.

"It's not that I am alone. I have my two boys who are currently in school. But yeah, sometimes it gets lonely."

"And where do you guys live?"

"Oh, we live just in the neighborhood in Mai-Ihi."

"And how long have you been friends with Morris?"

"Well, he was my college mate," he inquired as they sat for breakfast.

"Well, make yourselves at home."

Alfonso had finished his cup of tea and slice of bread when he spotted a gaming machine. He requested permission to play it with his friend so they could kill time.

"Yeah, go on," the friend allowed.

They decided to play car racing and agreed that whoever won would interact with a girl from the neighborhood.

They started with Tony leading for about six hundred meters while Alfonso was trying all he could to speed up. With about five hundred meters to go, he accelerated, overtaking Tony.

"Well! Well! Well! Who was talking here?"

"Maybe we should play another one. I don't concede."

"No, our deal."

So they went to their host.

"Sir..."

"Call me Mr. Kelvin."

"Oh nice, Mr. Kelvin. We would like to tour the neighborhood."

"Well, how soon? You have not even stayed an hour, and you guys want to leave?"

"Actually, we had a deal that whoever won the racing match would get a chance to interact with a girl from the neighborhood."

"Okay, but be vigilant."

Barely had they walked a hundred meters when they saw someone familiar.

There was an empty shop just next to them.

"Hey, Tony, I don't think we are safe."

The guy had three other men with bats.

"Let's hide in here," Tony suggested.

It was Morris, and he had three other boys with him who had, by then, approached the shop.

"When we find that Tony guy and his counterpart, we'll teach them a lesson," Morris said as they passed near the shop. "I know they are the ones who killed James." (James was among the people that Alfonso and Tony had slain.) "I know for a fact."

"Let me ease myself in this shop," one of the gang members decreed.

Upon entering the shop, he saw Tony. He yelled and signaled the others as they came in. The two wrecked havoc on them as they cried in pain. They tried, but they were overpowered, and Morris' side was completely routed.

The two turned to Morris, still breathing heavily.

"You had been a good friend…"

"Please… spare me."

"Well! Did you consider this while conspiring against us? Good riddance!" Alfonso evoked as he saw a knife nearby.

Morris had been spectating all this time, hoping that his side would win.

"We can talk this over," he persuaded Alfonso as he knelt. His hands trembled like a feeble twig, but Alfonso was having none of it.

He requested Tony to tilt Morris' neck, and he ruptured him without hesitation.

One of the instigators saw what was happening. He secretly retrieved his phone, took a photo, and sent a message to his brother:

"I had gone for a mission which has failed, and I am about to be killed. Please avenge my death."

Both of them butchered the other three as payback.

Immediately, Mr. Kelvin appeared and spotted some people on the ground. He was buffeted and approached the scene, wanting to find out what had happened.

"Oh my goodness! What is happening here, Alfonso? Is this Morris? You guys better tell me what has happened."

He went and held Morris' body with strength depleted. His eyes were heavy as Tony explained.

"Honestly, sir, we were engaging in a conversation with Morris, telling us how sorry he had been for being rude to us when all of a sudden, these three goons appeared and stabbed him.

Tony was quick enough to see the bats hidden in this empty shop, and we used them. But on realizing that they would overpower us, we grabbed the knife and brought them down. It was a heated ordeal.

I am sorry, but we'll have to leave."

So they left, with Mr. Kelvin wailing on the ground as they headed to Tony's house.

"That was swift for real! I must commend you," Tony engaged Alfonso.

A phone call—it was Kingsley.

Immediately, Alfonso saw it; he hung up.

A message dropped.

"Hi, Alfonso. I know you are going through a lot, but I just want you to know that I am human, too, and for uncle's memory, I forgive you."

He jumped in celebration as he engaged Tony, telling him that it was all good, that they could go ahead home with no worries.

"Wait, what?"

"Yes, Kingsley will no longer be heading to the police. We are free! At last!" Tony exclaimed.

They reached Alfonso's home and found Kingsley.

"Yooo, maaan… you are a he-goat."

"Call me a he-goat, but you have escaped by a whisker."

They all laughed.

"Mr. Malcolm said he will be coming over."

"Malcolm? Oh, what a nice surprise."

Malcolm arrived, bringing their favorite delicacy.

"Guys, I have brought you a favorite delicacy."

"Thanks… If only you knew what we've witnessed today."

"I would presume it's more deadly than last time…" he joked.

They shared the meal and bonded.

"Uncle, I believe that the people who assassinated my dad are still largely out there. At the very least, we should be cautious in everything we do."

"Very true! You have a point. Although we don't know who it is, we should be very careful."

"Thanks, Tony, for always being there for me. You are such a caring friend."

"Don't worry; friends are there for such times."

"You must be really lucky. Having friends who stick by you like Tony isn't something ordinary," Kingsley noted.

"That's why I'm always by his side."

"I declare the one who did that will pay dearly!" Malcolm confessed.

A phone call came in.

"Hello?"

"Hello, my name is Mr. Regan."

"Sorry, do I know you?"

"Oh, forgive my manners. I am Morris' dad, and I have received the news of my son's death. I am glad that you tried all you could to protect him from the goons who murdered him. It is with that regard that I am inviting you to his burial."

(It was a custom in their culture for the body to be laid to rest in three days.)

"Okay, I'll be there with my other friend."

He alerted Tony, but Tony could not make it since he had other commitments.

Days seemed to pass so fast, and it was already Thursday. Alfonso woke up early in the morning, took a shower, had breakfast, and then embarked on the journey to Regan's place.

Hundreds of mourners had gathered in their compound, and the late Morris' friends had convened to celebrate him while deliberating on the great loss they had suffered. They discussed how instrumental he had been in their lives and how they had never come across such a friendly person. Oh, it was a huge blow. They sang dirges as a somber mood engulfed the place.

During the sermon, the preacher regretted the actions that led to Morris' death. He acknowledged how his friends had tried to help him to no avail. He also emphasized what a loving and kind gentleman he had been. "May his soul rest in peace," he concluded. Cries of anguish were heard all over from Morris' relatives, while his father remained silent, deep in thought. When the time came to lay Morris to rest, his body was interred. The cries of grief intensified as his relatives became overwhelmed. Oh, and I had forgotten to mention—Morris had no mother; she had died in a tragic accident.

The event came to an end as mourners began departing to their respective homes.

Alfonso retreated to his home as the day came to an end.

The following day at ten a.m., Mr. Regan called. "Hey, can you come to my home immediately? I have good news I want to share."

"Oh, I can't wait," Alfonso replied.

So, he took a quick shower, dressed up, and headed to Regan's house.

When Alfonso arrived, he knocked on the gate, and Regan hurriedly came to open it. They walked slowly to the house as Regan expressed how instrumental Alfonso had been throughout the entire time.

"I have some news I wanted to share with you. Excited?"

"Yes! I'm kind of nervous—I don't know what it could be," Alfonso responded.

"I am the new director of John and John's Holdings, and I'll be collecting a hefty salary."

"Oh, that's excellent, I presume…" Alfonso began, but before he could finish, Mr. Regan continued.

"Would you like to celebrate this achievement with me?"

"Why not? Oh, that's really brilliant. So, what do you suggest?"

"That you come and start living with me—be like the son I will never have," Regan said.

Alfonso was delighted, and they gave each other a high five.

"Okay, sir, I promise to be as mindful as possible."

"Don't you worry," Regan reassured him. "So, just go and pick up your belongings and then come."

"Tomorrow, I suppose?"

"Yes, tomorrow."

Everything went as planned, and Alfonso bid farewell to his cousin and friend before leaving for Mr. Regan's house. Regan was overjoyed as he welcomed Alfonso and showed him his room. They engaged in a celebratory discussion, both enjoying their new arrangement.

"You know, you seem to be a great person. I could make you a benefactor to my properties, especially now that I have landed this big deal."

"And I assure you, I will be as loyal as possible," Alfonso promised.

To make himself useful, he took on small duties like mowing the lawn, cleaning, and running errands. Regan was pleased, and they began living together in harmony.

Alfonso's birthday was approaching, and Mr. Regan decided to throw him the best birthday party.

When the day arrived, all the preparations were underway. Mr. Regan invited all his good friends, along with two of Alfonso's cousins and Tony's brother.

A tent had been pitched in the compound, and guests began streaming in. Mercy, one of Regan's nieces, along with Kingsley, helped in the kitchen. They gathered ingredients to prepare pilau, nyama choma, and chapati.

Some guests arrived in a black Mercedes, and upon alighting, Regan recognized them and hurriedly rushed to welcome them.

"Welcome, Mayor!" (He was the former mayor, accompanied by his family.)

"Ah, it's nice to see you again, Regan. How have you been?"

"I've been okay. Thank you for making it to this occasion."

They conversed as Mr. Regan directed him to the guest area.

A friend of Regan's approached Alfonso.

"Nice to meet you. You're welcome," he said. "You should probably pay us a visit sometime, right? For Mr. Regan to host such a magnificent ceremony for you, you must be a really good person."

They both laughed as Alfonso led him to the guest area.

A large music system in the compound provided entertainment. People jammed to their favorite tunes, some standing to enjoy the music while others danced.

When it was time to feast, guests served themselves from a buffet.

Tony arrived with a big cake featuring Alfonso's picture on it.

"Attention! Attention! The moment we've all been waiting for—the reason for this party—has arrived. I'd like to invite Alfonso to come forward so that he can cut the cake," Regan announced.

Alfonso gave a short speech and concluded by expressing gratitude to Mr. Regan.

"I promise to love him forever and be the son he always wanted," he said.

He then took the knife and started cutting the cake.

"Happy birthday to you..."

The birthday song could be heard from afar when a latecomer arrived. Hungry, he headed straight to the food area to serve himself.

However, as soon as he saw Alfonso, he was stunned. Without hesitation, he hurried toward Mr. Regan.

"You invited me to this party, but if this is the celebrant, something is really off," he said.

"What do you mean, something is off?" Regan asked.

The man retrieved a photo of Alfonso that his brother had sent him and showed it to Regan.

"Alfonso?!!!" Regan exclaimed before collapsing to the ground.

The others, including Mr. Kelvin, rushed over to see what had happened, but Alfonso grabbed the photo and ran as fast as he could. Tony followed him.

They bolted out of the gate and found an unlocked car. They jumped in and sped off, with no clear destination in mind.

Immediately, Alfonso thought of an idea, and the boy whom they had helped from their uncle posed as a good exile—that's where they headed. Upon reaching the house, they had barely stayed for ten minutes before there was a knock. John, the boy, went to open the door, and it was five guests from the party.

"You idiot! They were following Alfonso, but he didn't know."

"You thought you would outsmart us? How could you?"

One of them contacted someone to find out whether Regan had regained consciousness. He learned that Regan had just woken up. He took some time, then called again to alert them that they had found Alfonso.

"Give me the directions..." He got them, then took a rifle from a neighbor who used it for safety purposes. He entered his car and headed to where Alfonso was.

Within no time, he arrived and banged the door open. Coincidentally, he found Alfonso being interrogated by the guests. He headed directly toward him and, just a few meters away, yelled,

"You are the most foolish idiot in this world! And today—oh, today—you are going to realize who you messed with!"

He fired at Alfonso. It was the worst nightmare Alfonso had ever experienced. He had been doing things however he wanted, but that was the end of it. As if in a scene from a movie, John jumped in front of Alfonso.

Kablam! The bullet lodged in him, leaving Alfonso gasping for air as if he had seen a ghost. Tony, who had taken a leave to go to the shop, suddenly appeared and saw everything that was happening.

"Alfonsooooo!!!"

Mr. Regan was about to fire a second shot when Tony pushed the gun slightly sideways, causing the bullet to miss. Immediately, he succeeded in snatching the rifle and threw Mr. Regan to the floor.

"Damn you!"

He shot him twice in both legs. Regan fell with a bang and was unable to move as blood oozed from his wounds.

Neighbors heard the commotion as Tony signaled to Alfonso, and they vanished.

"Hurry, let's go to your place. This rifle cannot stay at our home because of Kinsley and stuff, but you can keep it, right?"

"It's alright, no issues."

They covered it with Tony's shirt and left.

# Chapter| 2

Alfonso had gotten the sense that he had conquered. "I am exceptional, great, and nothing can bring me down." He focused on Kingsley, who was packing his bags. From the look of things, he wanted nothing to do with him.

"Traitor! Insolent! You are a disgusting, brutal murderer! I should have reported you at first, but now I have enough evidence."

"What do you mean you want to report me?"

"Is that a question? It sounds silly—that's obvious. I am going to report you, but better still, I will go back to my home."

As the debate was going on, Tony came into their house.

"Mr., I thought you were modest. How then can you be involved in such things?" Kingsley challenged him.

"You can never understand—even the fact that Mr. Regan wanted to kill my friend. So what would you have rather I did? If it wasn't for my intervention, he wouldn't be alive!"

As they were conversing, the boy who had set Alfonso up immediately called. (He had exchanged numbers during the party.)

"Hey, Kingsley."

"What's up?"

"I just wanted that beast of a guy calling himself Alfonso to apologize! Killing someone's child is not something to joke about!"

"Yes, I will insist, and he will. Thank you."

The phone call ended, and Kingsley immediately went straight to Alfonso.

"Damn you! Make an apology to Regan."

"Hey, listen to this loser." He reverted to Tony. "You think it's easy to be in our shoes? That will never happen."

Jack had come to pay a visit to Mr. Regan and had brought some shopping. He knocked, and Mercy opened the gate for him. Mr. Regan saw him from afar and quickly walked toward him with his crutches.

"Hello, sir. I am very sorry for your situation."

"Don't worry; at least it didn't render me crippled."

"Hey, I have someone from the scene where you were shot who can testify against that Alfonso guy."

"No need. I was also involved in shooting that guy."

"Oh, by the way, did the man who took the bullet survive?"

"I hear he is in the intensive care unit."

"That is not a police case. That one, I will handle myself with the full wrath that the situation requires."

"Can you get me one family member of that guy?"

"Oh, I am not really a bad person, but I don't know... maybe I can link you up with the kin of the other victims."

"Oh, sure."

"That man is really merciless."

"How are you coping with the injuries? And with the trauma?"

"Well, I am talking to Morris' friends, who are helping me celebrate his life."

"Things are not easy... as for the injuries, I have learned to cope with them."

He showed the picture once more. "Here, he slit his throat."

Mr. Regan looked in disbelief as he hardened his face and clenched his jaw. He couldn't imagine going through that kind of pain.

The two agreed that it was beneficial for them to spend more time together.

"It would be therapeutic for you."

Mercy was preparing a dish, and she came to set the dining table.

"How are things?" she asked Jack.

"Um... I am trying to cope... I will never regret what I did."

"Yes, you really saved us."

"Uncle, you must be really generous."

"Yes... do you guys want to spend some time on vacation?"

"Vacation?"

"Yes, yes, yes! I would be delighted. And you, Mercy?"

"Yes," she alluded.

"Okay, just make sure you send me pictures each day."

"No worries, Uncle."

"Yes, it will be a great reward for both of you, especially Jack. Meanwhile, give me the number of the people we agreed on."

"Okay, here you go." Jack gave him the number.

"So, I'll hire a domestic worker for those few days."

"Okay, sorted."

"Jack, you seem quite interesting."

"Oh, I am fun to be around. I promise you shall enjoy."

"So, which destination suits you most—the Maldives, Zanzibar, or the coast?"

"Maldives! Maldives! Maldives!" They both shouted in unison.

"Okay, Maldives you like, Maldives you will go."

Mercy went and hugged Regan, and Jack bowed to him and kissed his hand.

"Thank you very much."

"You are welcome. You pose more like a son to me."

"Thank you."

"So, here is the card. Go shop for whatever you may require as I book a hotel."

Jack was so happy that his efforts paid off.

"Yes, they did!" Mercy affirmed.

"Maldives, here we come!!!" Jack celebrated.

Within two hours, they had reached the central business district, drove further, and arrived at their favorite mall, where they planned to buy toiletries, bags for the trip, and other necessities. They spent about forty-five minutes and were done.

Next, they were to shop for the clothes to wear during the trip.

"What will you be wearing?" Mercy asked.

"Anything, provided it looks good on me. And you?"

"I'd like to wear tights and a bright top."

"Shall we?"

They picked about four pairs of clothes and paid for them. It cost about thirty-five thousand shillings. They felt optimistic.

"Thank you, Uncle. We've done what you told us. Now it's up to you."

"Okay, let's see. I've booked a hotel, so you guys book a flight, and off you go."

"Okay, Uncle."

So, they booked a flight for the coming Saturday. By then, it was Thursday.

Saturday arrived. They met early in the morning at around six at the airport and hugged each other.

"Shall we?"

They went to the waiting area as their flight was scheduled for eight a.m.

Finally, they enjoyed it! It was time! So they boarded and sat next to each other.

"Wow! It's going to be nice."

"Yes! Imagine if we hadn't gotten this opportunity. Just

imagine if we had gone to the local beach! I can't believe how constraining it would have been."

"All the way!!"

"We are about to take off," an air hostess announced as all the passengers grew excited.

"Ian, and you?"

"Jack."

"Oh, that's nice. Have you ever traveled with this airline before?"

"Never. This is actually my first time."

"Well, I've been on it a couple of times, and I prefer it to others."

"Oh, I see..."

Jack was talking to the passenger sitting next to him on the right.

"Going for a business trip, I suppose?" Jack asked.

"Yes, partially, but I'm going to meet an old friend of mine. It's more of an acquaintance catch-up, but we are still executing a deal."

"Oh, that's incredible. As for me, I'm going for a vacation."

"Oh! You really did pick the right destination. So, which hotel are you going to?"

"I'm going to Blue Whales Hotel."

"Ah! In my opinion, that's the best. You will be enjoying the sandy beaches and, in the evening, be treated to some nice delicacies. That's awesome."

The air hostess came to take their orders, and Tony and Mercy ordered fried rice with chicken and minced meat with pasta, respectively. The flight took eleven hours, and they finally landed at Velana International Airport.

The place was very striking, and Jack was mesmerized.

"Look at that! The people seem so cool. It's nothing like I've seen before."

"Can you see how everything looks orderly? It's so beautiful."

"I'm at a loss for words."

They went to the passport control desk, where their passports were checked. Immediately, a taxi approached, and the driver greeted them.

"Hi! May I be of service to you?"

"Sure."

The two boarded the cab.

"Take us to this location."

"Okay! We'll be there in three hours."

Jack was so excited!

"The moment I've been waiting for has arrived!" Jack exclaimed.

"In fact, let me call your uncle."

"Oh sure!"

"Hello!!!!"

"Yes, Jack?"

Jack expressed his happiness.

"Uncle, you are so kind. Thank you for enabling us to experience this thrilling adventure."

"Okay."

"The place is super elegant. The people are bright, and the atmosphere here is like nothing I've ever seen."

"Okay, that's fantastic. Here at home, someone came to replace Mercy, and from the look of things, she's doing a pretty good job."

"Yeah, let me first take a picture and send it to you as we pledged."

When they reached the hotel, they asked the driver to take a photo of the two at the entrance, which he gladly did. They were glowing, and their smiles—oh, let's not even talk about that! Jack sent the pictures.

"Wow!!!! Is this real?" Kinsley wondered.

(The photos were mistakenly sent to Kinsley.)

Mercy took Jack's phone as they went to their rooms and Jack didn't notice it.

"Wow!!! You look so bright," Kinsley was amazed.

"That's an overrated compliment."

"Not in any way! In fact, I'm planning to honor Jack for what he did."

"Ah! Benevolent! So, what will be the gift?"

"Let me not spoil the surprise. How many days are you staying there?"

"About three days."

"Okay. Let me put my plans in place."

Early the next morning, Kinsley rose very early and went to a law firm in Nairobi.

"Hi, my name is Kinsley, and I need your help..." he said to one of the lawyers he was assigned to consult.

"Okay, how can I be of help?"

"Well, a cousin of mine assured me that he will gift me his inheritance."

"Oh, that's splendid! How much are we talking about, or what properties are involved?"

"We are talking about five million."

"Okay. Where is the cousin?"

"Oh, he is in a coma, and I really need him to sign the document as soon as he wakes up."

"So, would you mind preparing the transfer document for me?"

"No issues. That's our work."

The lawyer went in and, within twenty minutes, was done.

"Here we go."

Kinsley paid the consultation fee and the charges for the will transfer document.

"Thank you."

"Hi, Alfonso."

"Oh, cousin, you're back?"

"Oh yes, I am. Would you mind us going for a beefed-up lunch today?"

"Oh, why not?"

"So, be ready. It will be a nice catch-up between the two of us, don't you think?"

"Sure, very brilliant of you."

Lunchtime arrived, and they went to their favorite chill spot in the CBD.

"What would you like?"

"Rice and beef."

"And you?"

"Oh, beef and ugali."

Within no time, the delicacies were brought, and the two focused on feasting.

It was a good time to catch up, and they talked about many things, including how life had slowly started gaining meaning and how they had to do their best to ensure it continued that way.

At about 3:45 PM, they left and immediately returned home. Alfonso lay on his bed and dozed off.

That was when Kinsley executed his plan. He woke Alfonso up and asked him to sign the document. Half-asleep, Alfonso didn't check what the document was about. Kinsley made sure he was steady just enough so that the signature looked exactly like the original one.

Immediately after, he left and went to the bank to present the document.

"You will have to come with the concerned person," the cashier asserted.

As Kinsley stood there stranded, someone appeared from the door leading to the bank staff's area.

"Ah! Mr. Charles."

"Oh, Kinsley..."

"It has been a very long time. How have you been?"

"Ah! I'm fine. And you look like a manager!"

"True, I am the manager."

"What!!!" Kinsley shouted in disbelief, celebrating the fact that he was just in time.

He explained his issue, and the manager instructed the staff not to delay him. The money was transferred into Kinsley's account.

(Mr. Charles was Kinsley's former headteacher.)

"Hello, can you connect me with Jack, please?" So Mercy handed the phone to Jack.

"Hi, Jack."

"Oh! Hello, Kingsley. Mercy told me that you had some joy in store for us..."

"Yes, you know, I've been thinking and just figured out that you need some token of appreciation for what you did. So here is the deal: give me your account number, and upon arrival, you will find a good portion of money in your account."

At first, Jack didn't know whether to believe him or not, but he gave him the benefit of the doubt.

"Mercy, Kingsley promised that he would be sending me a lump sum, but I am not certain if he is telling the truth..."

"So what would be his agenda?"

"Well, come to think of it, there is no reason to doubt him…" And that's when he burst into excitement, seeing that he would be favored.

Their trip lasted for three days. After sending some photos to Mr. Regan, they left the city and headed back.

"Oh my! How was the trip, son?"

"Fantastic." Mercy went and hugged him and couldn't let go of his chest. Jack, too, joined in, as if chicks huddling under their mother's wings.

"Where is the five million you took from me?" Alfonso had by now discovered. He asked authoritatively. (This had been the recently transferred inheritance to Alfonso's account.)

"I am the worst cousin. You brutally treated Jack and Morris… There is your reward," he asserted derogatorily.

"Okay…" He was speechless.

He went to his room, banged the door, and sat on the floor. Tears began to trickle down his face. The only means of survival he had left… He cried bitterly and couldn't believe what had happened. Pangs of fury filled him as he breathed heavily. His only share from his father! He yelled in disbelief and rolled on the floor.

Tony stormed in when he saw Alfonso lying on the floor. He was shocked and went to Kingsley.

"Kingsley, what has happened? What's wrong with Alfonso?"

Tony wondered.

"I really don't know! I am as shocked as you!"

He rushed back to Alfonso.

"Al! Al!" He went for a jug of water, poured some into a cup, and offered it to him.

"Al, what's wrong?"

By then, Alfonso had not regained his energy, so Tony gave him more and more water.

"What do you want?! Leave me!!" he shouted as his voice broke.

Alfonso became indifferent. "This is the last time I need you," he said, carried away by emotions.

"Alfonso, tell me what's up?"

"I don't need anyone's assistance."

Tony tried all he could, but Alfonso wasn't cooperating. It had been about an hour, and Alfonso hadn't yielded. That's when Tony gave up and left, hoping that Alfonso would come back to his normal state later.

The next day, Jack was taking his ten percent share to the church when Alfonso spotted him.

Immediately, he walked toward him and was just a few meters behind. Jack's shoelace had come undone, so he bent down to tie it and placed his duffle bag on the ground. At that moment, Alfonso picked it up.

Alfonso immediately went to Tony.

"Hello, hi, are you better?"

"Don't worry."

"Oh, so how can I be of help to you?"

"Yes, I need the rifle."

"What are you up to?"

"Oh, this is a special mission that I need to handle alone."

Within no time, Tony was there with the gun, carefully slid into a black bag.

"Thanks."

Tony was perturbed by Alfonso going on missions without him. When he questioned Alfonso, he paid little attention and left.

Alfonso couldn't come to terms with the fact that Jack had benefited from his rightful inheritance. That thought alone drove him mad.

So Alfonso set out to find a taxi, which was readily available.

The taxi driver smiled at Alfonso, and Alfonso smiled back.

Within no time, they were at the local bank.

The watchman approached, and upon seeing the driver, he came and opened the door.

He was more than pleased, and upon seeing Alfonso, he said, "Have a blast," as he opened the cab door.

Alfonso assembled his weapon and stormed into the bank. "Anyone who moves gets the first bullet!!!"

It was a confusing moment for everyone inside the bank. People were bewildered as Alfonso ordered them to lie on the ground.

A lady began screaming, and Alfonso pointed at her and blew her head off. People panicked as another person, who was close to him, collapsed.

"That was a demonstration to all of you," he declared.

He then went to a man lying next to him and pointed the rifle at him.

"Are you courageous enough?"

The man shook his head in fear as tears trickled down his face.

"Cool."

After going to the counter, he directed the cashier to fill the bag, and the terrified cashier did so.

Alfonso gladly ran back to the cab, which sped off quickly.

About thirty minutes later, Alfonso approached Tony's gate.

He hooted, but no one came out. He hooted again, but still, no one came. Just as they were about to leave, Tony appeared, his face slightly dull.

Alfonso hysterically shouted at him as the two started celebrating after Alfonso explained what had happened and showed him the cash from the robbery.

Tony was utterly flabbergasted. He lifted his counterpart in joy as they celebrated.

The three then drove to Alfonso's home.

"For you to keep your mouth shut, I'll give you a hundred thousand."

"No, a hundred thousand is too little."

Kingsley was a well-behaved man—but not when it came to money. He agreed to keep silent for one hundred and fifty thousand.

He took the money and immediately left to enjoy at least some of the proceeds.

He retreated to a hotel near the bank and sat down. Just then, he overheard a waiter talking on the phone about the robbery.

When she ended the call, she began describing the horrific scene of the lifeless bodies Alfonso had killed.

Kingsley requested her to send him the photos, which she gladly did.

After having his late lunch, he returned to find them packing the cash.

"Guys, did you have to go to this extent?" "Yes! Because someone decided to steal my inheritance. Oh, and I am quite aware that you gave Jack some of my money."

Kingsley was intimidated and had to change the topic.

"So guys, now here's the plan..." Alfonso was giving directives when the driver requested to use the restroom.

As he came out, something shocking happened—he zoomed in on a picture on Kingsley's (who, by then, was in the kitchen) phone and was utterly shaken.

It was his cousin, Dennis.

Panic filled him as he gasped for air and immediately left the house.

A deep sense of despair and grief engulfed him. He felt confused and couldn't believe that he had contributed to his cousin's death.

Dennis had been his everything.

How could he?!

Regret consumed him as he felt completely defeated.

He got into his cab and drove to the bank scene.

Everyone was restless. An ambulance had arrived and was ferrying casualties to the hospital. Police had drawn the yellow tape.

Immediately, he received a call from his brother.

"Hello, Dennis."

"Hi, Mark… Finally, my actions have caught up with me," he yelled.

"Dennis, you don't have to blame yourself."

His voice cracked as it became fainter. (Alfonso had killed two others.)

"Miracle's stomach has been badly ruptured by a bullet… He has been admitted to the national hospital."

"It's okay…"

Dennis ended the call, wiping his tears.

"It's okay, Miracle… It's okay."

The police were assessing the scene.

"No possible way that I'll take this cross alone! I will do something to that guy!"

"This is too much for me..."

"Sir! Sir!!" He approached one officer.

"Please, I need your cooperation..."

"What kind of cooperation do you need? Speak, I'm listening..."

"Okay, sir," he talked as he shook. "You have to give my cousin justice!" he spoke as he wiped his tears.

The officers became more attentive.

"Sir, he has killed my cousin. Look, there is his blood," he illustrated as he pointed to where his cousin's body lay in the picture. "You have to arrest the perpetrator. Let me show you where he lives—you might find him."

Dennis was saturated with vengeance.

The officer excused himself so that he could concentrate on what he was being led to.

"Please follow me," Dennis insisted.

The police, filled with curiosity, took his patrol car as they set off on the journey.

(Dennis had told him that he arrived immediately after the robbery had happened and that his cousin was waiting for him. As his cousin struggled to breathe in his last moments, he told him that the shooter was a man who lived next to their shop at Mai-Ihi, and that's where he was taking him.)

It was a one-hour drive, and on the way, Alfonso called Malcolm, who was the cop on duty. Dennis heard the call and was confused, but he overruled his suspicion, assuming it was another Alfonso.

"Hello, Uncle. Where are you?"

"Hi, nephew. Is everything alright? I'm on a mission."

"Yeah... I want to tell you something. I hope you don't take it the wrong way."

"What is it, Alfonso?"

"I have seven million, and it isn't mine..."

Considering the dynamics of Alfonso's life, he excused himself from the vehicle for privacy purposes.

"THE SEVEN MILLION...!" The thought rang in Malcolm's head. By then, there was a hint that the same seven million

Alfonso had mentioned was the same amount that had been stolen. Plus, the journey was headed to his residence...

He suddenly cut the call and rushed to Dennis to inquire further. But Dennis had realized everything—that the person he intended to have arrested, Alfonso, was his uncle. Out of frustration, he stepped out, realizing that his plan would not succeed.

Malcolm went directly to Alfonso's home and professionally removed his handcuffs.

"You Are Under Arrest For The Murder Of Innocent Civilians And Bank Robbery!"

Immediately, Alfonso became teary, and Malcolm was filled with sympathy.

He returned to the crime scene as the other officer, whom Malcolm had alerted, wanted to know what the lead was. But he asserted that it was negative.

Next was the press briefing.

"Hello, Officer Malcolm. Do you think you can offer a press briefing on today's incident? We know you are the right man!"

He agreed, thanking the heavens for that leverage, seeing that he would keep everything undercover.

"Good afternoon, ladies and gentlemen. It is with deep sadness and concern that we, as the police, condemn today's killings. This matter is being taken very seriously by our team, and investigations are fully underway. We assure the public that we will bring the involved criminal to justice. Thank you, and may our country remain great."

On arriving home, Dennis took a warm shower and retired to bed.

At that moment, he received a call from an unknown number. Upon answering, the caller was a girl who seemed quite excited.

"Hello."

"Hi... You know what? Miracle and I had an affair, and guess what? I'm expecting his baby. I'd like you to..."

Before she could finish, Dennis intercepted, "I'm so sorry." He sighed heavily as he delivered the news.

"I don't know how you are going to take this, but I have some bad news."

The lady immediately changed her tone, becoming more serious.

"Bad news? What could it be?"

"My cousin is in a very critical condition, and I don't think he will make it."

Confused by the news, the lady burst into uncontrollable tears, bargaining for her baby daddy's wellness.

He mentioned the hospital and the ward, and immediately, she took off for the said hospital.

On reaching, the doctor was briefing Miracle's family. As she drew near, she received the devastating news—Miracle had passed away.

She could not process the information. She rolled on the floor, crying in anguish.

# Chapter| 3

So, they had already buried Miracle, and it was the next week. It happened that Agnes was at her home, and Dennis was passing by. He called her.

"Hey, hello, I'm currently at Pumwani stage. Where is your home?"

"Oh, take the straight road you see at the stage, walk for about a hundred meters, then turn left. When you get there, call me."

"Okay," he agreed.

They connected as Dennis showed delight at meeting her, and they headed to her home. They bonded, and Dennis initiated a conversation on the issue of interest.

"I just have the right plan."

"Right plan? I don't get you," Agnes declared.

"Look, we are going to teach that donkey that killed your husband a lesson!"

At the mention of the subject, Agnes clenched her jaw as it was painful for her.

"You know the person that killed him?" she reacted in shock.

"Yes, I happened to be near the robbery scene, and I saw him come out. I recognized his face."

"It's okay… he took away the greatest gift in my life," she said. "I desire that we orchestrate a revenge move. Are you in?"

"Why not? I'd like him to face the most intensified pain."

"This is the thing—I looked for his number. We'll call him, pretend to have an occasion, and invite him. When he comes, we'll swindle all the money he collected in the robbery at gunpoint."

"I don't need the money, but if it makes him sad… I'm in."

"After that, we'll blindfold him, drive him to an unknown location, and dump him there."

So, Dennis called him.

"Hello, Alfonso."

"Hello, who is this?"

"It's Dennis."

"Oh, how are you?"

"Fine, I just wanted to invite you to a small get-together I'm having with my coursemates."

"I thought you'd enjoy it."

"Oh? When will it take place?"

"The day after tomorrow. I will give you the directions."

"Well, there's nothing I'm doing. I bet I can make it."

"Nice, okay, you are so welcome. Try to make it by ten-thirty because of some key agendas we have for the meeting."

"That's okay."

It was Thursday already—the agreed day for the purported party. Alfonso woke up that morning, had breakfast, and then got ready to head to the agreed location. He was excited; he would finally be unwinding after such crazy incidents.

"Hello, Dennis."

"Oh! Hi, Alfonso."

"I'm at the stage."

"Okay, give me some minutes."

Dennis went to pick him up, and they went to the house. They convinced him that he was the first one to arrive and pretended to be cooking just to trick him. In thirty minutes, the two went to the sitting room.

"Alfonso!!! Alfonso!!! Alfonso!!!"

Immediately, Alfonso noticed the change in Dennis' demeanor, and he begged to excuse himself.

"Why would you step out from the scene that was meant for you?!"

Alfonso panicked. He looked around for anything he could use as a weapon.

"Looking for something?"

Dennis removed a pistol as Alfonso began to shake.

"You killed my husband! I am pregnant with his baby! In your endeavor to rob the bank… and now… NOW IT'S MY TURN!" Agnes loudly declared.

"Now we are going to have a small party here."

Alfonso was confused.

"We are going to require you to transfer all the cash in your account through your phone to my account."

Alfonso was dumbfounded. He felt a deep sense of regret. He could not believe that he had been played—first his inheritance, then his money from the robbery, despite the high-level skill he had employed to get it.

"SHIIIEEET!!" he yelled.

Oh, that was the worst debilitation! This was not over. He knew very clearly—they just didn't know who they were messing with.

So, they took him to a mobile money shop, and he reluctantly entered his PIN to transfer the money to another number and they returned home.

He sat quietly, not knowing what to do, as the two hugged each other in celebration.

"In fact, this can be instrumental in raising my kid," Agnes continued celebrating.

"Now, you are as useless as lips on a chicken… You have no use to us."

Alfonso clenched his fist, ready to throw a punch, but the other lady had the gun pointed at him.

"Arrrghhh!" Alfonso screamed.

They blindfolded Alfonso, tied his hands, drove to Kiserian, and dropped him there.

He managed to untie himself and remove the blindfold. Feeling down and with a low spirit, he approached a guy he had spotted.

"Hey, my name is Alfonso, and I really need your help."

The man lent him his phone, and that's when he called Tony.

"Tony!!!!" His voice broke. "Tony!!! Imagine—they have swindled all the money."

"Alfonso! Is that you? Oh, stop crying. What has happened? Calm down and tell me…" Tony consoled him and agreed to meet him after he arrived home.

"So, is this a stranger's phone? How do I send you the fare?"

The stranger overheard the conversation.

"Let me talk to him," he interjected Alfonso as he offered his condolences.

"Don't worry, I'll give him the needed fare."

"Oh, thank you so much. That would really help."

So, the stranger ensured Alfonso got to the right matatus going to town and gave him a thousand shillings.

"This will be enough for you to reach Kiambu."

"Thank you so much," Alfonso expressed his gratitude as he left for the stage.

It was about a two-hour journey, and he reached home, where he met Kingsley.

He greeted him but didn't tell him what had happened. About thirty minutes had passed when two police officers stormed into their house.

"ALFONSO! Where the hell is ALFONSO?" they asked assertively.

Kingsley, who was watching TV, was astonished. At that moment, Alfonso came out of the bedroom to drink water, unsuspecting, and the two officers grabbed him and handcuffed him.

Alfonso was bewildered. He watched as his face became pale. He tried to defend himself to no avail as the officers left with him. They went inside the police van as he thought hard.

"What a misfortune. First, all my cash is taken, and now this..."

Alfonso was having the worst day. While all this was happening, Kingsley called their uncle Malcolm to brief him on what had happened.

"Finally! It's catching up with him," Malcolm exclaimed, leaving Kingsley confused, not knowing what to do.

"Finally, Alfonso, your days are over. Now you are going straight to jail," Alfonso castigated himself.

They took him and placed him in a cell inside the station. One of the inmates showed excitement at Alfonso's arrival, who was uneasy. Apparently, one of the witnesses in the robbery had reported Alfonso, leading to his arrest.

"So what brings you here?" the inmate questioned.

"Well, I was involved in a bank robbery and killed quite a number of people. I guess that's why I am here," he responded innocently.

"As for me, I raped a lady who had dressed provocatively, and I was traced after some people told on me."

"And this happens exactly after I have been robbed of my seven million."

"What!... Seven million? That sounds like a lot of money."

"Yeah, exactly—the money I stole from the bank."

"What?! Then you are lucky. Now they have no evidence. Once they put you on trial, they can't find you guilty if the stolen cash was deposited in your account since it is no longer there. If indeed you erased the message, you can argue that you are innocent based on that single fact."

"That's still risky because they can always check the bank records, and that will incriminate me."

"Which bank are you in?"

"Messengers Bank."

"Oh! Oh! Oh! Is there anyone luckier than you?"

"What do you mean?"

"I mean, my brother works in that bank. I'll make a call to him. After you give me your account number, I will ask him to erase all the transactions from the day you stole the money."

Alfonso's face brightened up.

"You are the most friendly person I've ever met. Thanks!"

He had gotten the much-desired reprieve.

"Oh... I am free!!!" he shouted, as all the other cellmates gazed at him in shock.

The cellmate went to the guard, who was his friend, and asked for his phone. Alfonso gave him his account number and the date he transferred the stolen cash. The cellmate called his brother, explained the situation, and his brother promised to clear the transaction, though he admitted he had to use the backdoor. The cellmate thanked him.

"With that, if you find a good lawyer, you can win the case and secure your freedom."

"That's it! That's it! Thank you so much!"

Later, another guard came and gave Alfonso a phone as required by the law. Alfonso dialed Kingsley's number, and he picked up.

"Hello..."

"Hello, cousin. Oh, I'm really sorry. How are you?" Kingsley asked uncertainly.

"I am well, and I have a slight chance of surviving."

"Yeeees!!" Kingsley exclaimed in relief.

"At least, Alfonso."

"Please book me an experienced lawyer so they can defend me. I guess my case will be heard next Monday, so make sure you are done with the arrangements by tomorrow."

"Oh, don't you worry. Leave that to me. I'll ensure that by Sunday, the lawyer will have come to familiarize himself with your case."

"Phew," Alfonso felt relieved.

Monday arrived, and Alfonso had confirmed that his court hearing was that day. His lawyer had visited him on Sunday, and they were ready.

"All rise," the judicial assistant commanded as the judge entered the courtroom. Everyone bowed, and the judge sat down as the case began.

The judge started by reading the accusations against Alfonso.

"Mr. Alfonso Balitoa, you are accused of shooting and killing three people, injuring others, and stealing a sum of seven million Kenyan shillings. Do you plead guilty as charged?"

"No, Your Honour."

"Okay," the prosecutor alluded.

"Can I call the first witness?"

A middle-aged lady appeared.

"Mrs. Nzioka, would you testify against the accused?"

"Yes, Your Honour. On the seventh of this month, I was at Marioshoni Bank when this individual stormed in with a rifle and ordered everybody to lie on the ground. He then shot a woman who tried to resist and, in the process, injured many others.

He proceeded to order the cashier to put money in a bag he was holding and disappeared, leaving the rest of us in panic and anguish."*

"Accused, do you wish to defend yourself against these accusations?"

"With what has just been said, at this point, I'd like to call my lawyer."

The lawyer stepped in.

"So, they are accusing my client, who is innocent. Madam, you are saying that the man in the picture ordered the money to be put in a bag?"

"Yes, it's true."

"About how much was placed in that bag?"

"I can't estimate."

"But it was a huge sum, right?"

"Yeah, it was a lump sum."

"Okay, so I would like to ask the prosecution to check the balance of my client's bank account or any other friend close to him to confirm that no amount whatsoever was deposited. This rules out the possibility of my client being guilty. Because if indeed he stole the money, at some point, he would have deposited it."

"That is all, Your Honour."

"Any more witnesses?"

"No, Your Honour."

"Case adjourned!" The judge banged his gavel.

"We'll meet at noon."

"All rise."

Everybody rose as people dismissed. Alfonso felt relieved and was even happier to see his close relatives, including Kingsley. They left the court and were to return in the afternoon.

Alfonso met with his lawyer and congratulated him on the defense. His odds of being released were high.

Time passed, and at two, everybody convened in the courtroom.

"All rise," the judge entered, and everyone stood up.

"I have come to the conclusion that Alfonso is innocent. Records from Messengers Bank show that he has never transacted with a figure higher than five thousand, which rules out the probability of him robbing a bank. If he had stolen the money, he would, by now, be enjoying a new life by withdrawing or sending large amounts of money. I, therefore, declare him innocent!" The judge banged his gavel.

All three of Alfonso's relatives broke into a pompous celebration as their kin would not be spending part of his lifetime in prison. They waited outside as Alfonso was given back his clothes and phone.

"Alfonso, I know you are innocent. I know you have gone to dangerous extents, but robbing a bank? They were simply picking faults with you. You would never dare do that."

"Yes, Auntie, I was relaxing with my friend that day. All in all, I am innocent!"

As Alfonso walked out, he approached Kingsley and gave him a fervent hug.

"Oh! Thank you for finding me a good lawyer."

"Don't worry. I'm always by your side."

So they parted ways, Kingsley and Alfonso going together, while everyone else left separately.

Kingsley took his time to prepare Alfonso's best dish while Alfonso engaged Tony on the phone about how narrowly he had escaped imprisonment.

"I'm sorry I did not make it to witness the case, as I had to attend to my mother, who was very sick in the hospital."

"How is she now?"

"Oh, she has improved tremendously."

"Okay, best friend, I'm happy that you are always here to support me."

Tony accepted the compliments as he expressed the same.

"Don't be worried; I've always got your back, through thick and thin."

"Thank you once more, even though our lives seem as if they are a scene from a movie."

"Thank you too, Alfonso..."

The phone call ended. Late lunch had already been prepared, and Kingsley was serving it. They ate to their satisfaction. As Alfonso celebrated seeing his freedom again, he went for sodas and came back with four of them.

It was in the evening, and Alfonso was reflecting on the direction his life had taken. He was quite upset.

What if I had gone to jail? How would Mommy and Daddy have perceived it from wherever they are? What would have become of our family? What would become of my fate?

Immediately, a thought about his lawyer ran through his mind.

I will call my lawyer. Maybe he can relate to my pain and shed more light on the situation.

So he called the lawyer.

"Hello."

"Hi, Alfonso..."

"Hello, Mr. Phillip?"

"How is everything? How are you coping at home? How is everybody? What are they saying was the reason for your arrest?"

"Funny enough, I have not met with any neighbor, and it has just bothered me—what would have happened if I was jailed? It saddens me that my life has taken such an unfortunate turn and that I have become a cold, inconsiderate being because that is not who I was..."

"Oh! So you are saying that you are sorry?"

"Yes, sir... I'm really touched by the grievous actions I've taken that have led to the loss of lives and injuries."

"Okay, can I come tomorrow so we can discuss this?"

"Okay, sure."

Alfonso slept, waiting for the following day. He had many expectations as he looked forward to finding answers to his biggest mysteries. The lawyer called, confirming that he would be at Alfonso's home by eleven a.m., so Alfonso had no choice but to wait.

Within no time, he arrived.

"Hello..."

"Oh! Mr. Phillip, welcome."

"Wow! I must admit, you have a nice house."

"Thank you."

"What will you be drinking—tea or coffee?"

"Oh, don't mind, just bring water."

"Okay."

Alfonso handed him a glass as he settled on the couch.

"So, Alfonso, I thought critically about your situation yesterday, and I would just recommend that you mention all the wrong things you've done."

"Really?!! I've done a lot of heinous and insensitive things. For example, upon finding out that my whole family had been murdered and witnesses had gathered in our home, I decided to slaughter every single witness, believing that they were the ones who killed them."

Mr. Phillip shook his head, contemplating the gravity of the matter.

"Then, there was this one time when I was invited by a friend called Regan to live with him. I just carried myself as expected until one day, when he held a very big party for me, and all his good friends attended. It was all colorful. All of a sudden, a man entered as a latecomer and went straight to him after noticing everything. He pulled out a video of me executing his son in the most brutal manner. Honestly, I felt it was very unfair. Even though I never regretted it, it has always been in my mind. Imagine—the man had even told me that I could be a beneficiary of his properties. And now, there's the bank robbery."

"Gosh!! You really have caused a lot of pain with your recklessness... So, are you willing to do something about it?"

"Yes, that's my greatest intention because, honestly, if I continue on the same path, it will end badly for me. That's where I need you. At least you are noble and can advise me on the way forward."

"Okay, here is my advice: First, go to all the people you've hurt and start by making apologies. I know, in some cases, it will be difficult, but don't worry—you can always go with a sum of money and offer it to the victims so that they will at least be more at ease. Also, watch out because that might result in injuries due to anger from the other parties. After that, please change your circle of friends and choose new ones who are not used to violence. Also, watch your anger."

"Yes...!"

Alfonso seemed quite excited about the suggestions and felt they were just the amends he needed.

The lawyer cheered. "That will make you a better individual who can relate to anyone. And one more thing—apologize to your relatives and let them know that bitterness was the original cause of all this, but now you have outgrown it and intend to live a life of purpose and consideration for others. Be constantly in touch with them and spend some quality time together."

Still, the lawyer was baffled at the extent of Alfonso's deviation.

"So, I'll be leaving now..."

"Thank you so much... I don't know where I would have gotten that advice from."

Alfonso expressed his gratitude.

"And where is Kingsley?" the lawyer asked curiously.

"Oh, he went to sort out some bills, but I'll greet him on your behalf."

"Nice."

"See you next time."

"Okay, let me see you off."

Alfonso walked him to the gate and thanked him again.

"I'll let you know how it goes."

"Well, thank you."

It was about five p.m. when Kingsley arrived.

"Hey, cousin, I've made up my mind..."

"Made up your mind? About what?"

"That the life I'm living is too hectic, and I need to change my ways!"

Kingsley was flabbergasted.

"Alfonso!!!!! Are you serious?"

"Yes, I'm serious."

"Oh, Alfonso, you've really made me proud..."

He sat down and began to cry. It was an emotional moment for him. His cousin had deviated in the most disastrous of ways, and now he had reverted back to his original nature.

"How wonderful... I've waited for this for the longest time—when you would come back to your senses. When you would stop being an animal. Oh, goodness, thank you, Alfonso... Thank you so much..."

Alfonso, too, shed a tear, overwhelmed.

The following day, it was time.

I shall go to everyone I have harmed and convey my apologies.

He headed to the first neighbor, who welcomed him. They had started conversing when Alfonso paused for a minute.

"Do you miss your brother?"

She started crying.

"I was the one who killed him."

It was like a lightning strike. The lady held Alfonso's shirt in bitterness as she processed what she had just heard. She stormed into the house.

"Risper! Risper!"

She suddenly returned with a knife. Just as she drew close to Alfonso, he ran away, fleeing from the compound.

"What have I just seen?"

He couldn't believe it. He decided to take a break and stopped by a shop.

"You are not permitted to come here, and I don't want to ever see you again!!!" someone shouted.

"Mr. Regan, I, I, I... Please hear me out," Alfonso pleaded.

Regan came out of the shop and drove him away by force.

Alfonso had no choice but to return home. He entered his bedroom, overcome with shame and pain. His voice started cracking.

Now he thinks I'm the old Alfonso, yet I've changed my ways. This is so unfair...

He began crying uncontrollably. Kingsley heard him and rushed to his room, pausing at the door.

You mean Alfonso is crying? This is remarkable...

Kingsley recorded a clip of him.

Suddenly, there was a loud bang in the sitting room. They were both alert. Two rough-looking men, who appeared to be police officers, took Alfonso and handcuffed him.

"You are under arrest for the murder of Morris Aseli and three other men. Anything you say will be used against you in a court of law..."

Kingsley was overly shocked. Mr. Regan had finally reported Alfonso to the police.

They arrived at Kikuyu Police Station, where his handcuffs were removed, and he was thrown into the cell. *Again, the same old process...* he thought. This time around, the cellmates looked unfriendly, as his immediate neighbor gave him a rigid stare and wanted nothing to do with him. The others seemed rough and cared little about him.

That night was one hell of a night; his head would not be still. Of course, the odds of him surviving this time were minimal, and there was no way he was going to escape the wrath of the law, especially with evidence proving he had committed the murder. *Oh my!!* This was worse than he had thought, and from the logistics, it was clear that this meant a life sentence.

That night, Alfonso couldn't sleep. That's when a friend approached him and greeted him.

"Hi, I've noticed that you have been quiet since you came..."

"Oh, that's true. I'm just in disbelief over what has transpired... Yes, I was arrested this afternoon by the very person from whom I was supposed to ask for forgiveness."

He paused for a moment as a teardrop ran down his cheek.

"You don't have to worry. Such is life. You only have to be positive and courageous, okay?"

"I'll try... Imagine, what if I had conveyed my apologies before he reported me?"

"Oh, I'm telling you, now is not the time for regrets. You are a good man, and you will get what you deserve; you deserve to be free, not incarcerated."

"And what about you?"

"As for me, I'm totally innocent. My brother connived against me."

"Oh, sorry. At least together, we can strengthen each other, can't we?"

"Yeah, that's true."

"Okay, sleep now. We need to rest."

"Okay, sleep well."

"Good night."

That night, Alfonso dreamt that Tony had joined him after the police questioned him about his residence. They were so rough that he could not lie, and that was exactly what transpired the following day.

It was a shock when Tony kept silent about Alfonso. He neither greeted him nor acknowledged his presence. That only added to Alfonso's pain. Tony, on the other hand, seemed to be getting along with most of the cellmates. There was one in particular who befriended him.

"Hey," he called out to Tony.

"Hi, I saw that the guy who came yesterday tried to approach you, but you acted uninterested..."

"Oh, you noticed?"

"You must really be keen. Yeah, I'm here because I always followed and did what favored him. I've never thought about it, but this is the place of reckoning. I'm informed that the reason for our arrest is a murder we committed against four people, and I'm sure that will cost me dearly."

"So, what's your stance on being here together?"

"I see it as the biggest blunder and can't bring myself to talk to him."

"What's the worst thing that could happen if you spoke to him?"

"Oh, I would feel betrayed."

"And don't you think you're in this together?"

He paused, then nodded. "Yeah, you have a point."

So Tony approached Alfonso and offered him his hand, and with a smile, Alfonso shook it.

"Hey, hi. What happened?"

Alfonso was still confused about how to tell him that he had changed and didn't know how to approach it. "I'm really sorry for putting you through this..." Tony paused for a moment, then sighed, saying he was okay with everything. He had accepted their fate and believed they deserved it.

A year passed as their case was being heard, and finally, the day of their verdict arrived. They had been taken to remand, and now they stood in court. The room was silent as a pin. The judge sat on the bench and, with utmost precision, delivered the verdict.

"The two suspects before the court have been found guilty of first-degree murder, and each suspect is sentenced to life imprisonment."

The entire courtroom erupted—relatives of Tony and Alfonso burst into wailing and tears, unable to believe what had just happened. Alfonso's entire life flashed before his eyes, while Kingsley was engulfed in instant bitterness, knowing the state of Alfonso's heart at the arraignment.

"All rise," the judge ordered as the session was dissolved.

Alfonso and Tony were escorted to the police Land Rover, waiting to take them to Kamiti Maximum Prison, as the courtroom watched in disbelief...

# Chapter| 4

It was a special occasion at Kamiti Maximum Prison as the governor of Kiambu had visited. He was led down the aisle of the prison when he came across Alfonso's cell and was eager to know more about him. That's when the warden explained the reality of the audio that Kingsley had recorded, which moved the governor to empathy. He immediately ordered Alfonso to be called.

"Yes, you..."

"Me?" Alfonso reacted with a mixture of excitement and uncertainty.

"Yes," the governor affirmed as he hurriedly approached the door, his heart pounding heavily.

"I understand that you have expressed intentions to apologize for the actions that led to your incarceration."

Alfonso could not believe his ears. This was the most benevolent thing he had heard in the entire time he had been imprisoned.

"Yes, that is true. I had decided to transform before the misfortune befell me."

"Ah! I see, then, that this act was somewhat unfair. I want to pardon you from your sentence so that you can cultivate your nature. You see, that kind of nature is what we all need to have."

"Okay, thank you very much!" Alfonso was boiling with joy, but he did not want to express it too much, fearing the favor might be revoked.

They walked towards the administration block, and in no time, Alfonso had been released.

Soon, Kingsley arrived to pick Alfonso up.

"Alfonso!!!!!!!"

They hugged each other as Kingsley shed some tears.

"Oh, look at you!" Alfonso cried heavily as he rested on his cousin's shoulder.

"It is well," Kingsley assured him as they began their journey back home.

That's when, coincidentally, Karanja met Alfonso. Alfonso was sitting on the grass, taking a walk near their home, when Mr. Karanja noticed him. As he was approaching, he overheard Alfonso lamenting on his phone.

"Oh, imagine, on that fateful day, I had gone to buy some milk at the shop when I met Mr. Regan. He prohibited me from buying from that shop again, and all along, his intentions towards me were unclear. He followed me slowly, and after realizing where I lived, he called the police on me. Imagine, coincidentally, I was planning on apologizing to him for the pain I had caused him before he reacted. But they convicted me and sentenced me to life imprisonment."

"What!! My uncle is so mean! I assume that if he had understood, he would have accepted an apology. So he can inflict that much pain just because I allowed him to run my shop while I went home to pick my charger? I will give him his due reward," he thought to himself.

Immediately, he went to the Alliance stage and took a matatu to Kinoo, where Mr. Regan resided. He passed by a shop, bought a liter of oil and a matchbox, and proceeded to jump into his uncle's compound. He spilled the oil around the base of the walls, except for the front part, and after lighting the matchstick, placed it on the walls, setting the house ablaze.

The fire grew larger and larger, and by the time Mr. Regan woke up, it was already raging.

He fell into shock and panicked as the smoke filled his room, making him choke. He anxiously called for help as the fire approached. Breathing became difficult.

"Reegaaan!!! Mr. Reeeegannn!"

"Yes! Please help!"

That's when a neighbor rushed in, covered in a wet blanket, and carefully pulled Mr. Regan out of the house. Phew! They escaped by a whisker.

The fire brigade arrived and began the process of extinguishing the flames.

Meanwhile, one of the paramedics who arrived with the ambulance had actually been a guest at the party Mr. Regan had set up for Alfonso. He was undoubtedly convinced that the incident had some ill intentions behind it.

They carried Mr. Regan on a stretcher, sirens blaring as they hurriedly passed through traffic.

Upon reaching the hospital, he was taken to the emergency unit and admitted.

The paramedic made a call to Mr. Kelvin, and they agreed to meet later that day. When they met, he expressed his concerns, suspecting that there was foul play involved in the misfortune that had befallen their friend. They decided to consult further with another party guest to reach a solid conclusion.

That's when they all unanimously agreed to have Alfonso apprehended on allegations that he was the one who had set Mr. Regan's house on fire, suspecting malice—just as he had allegedly killed his son.

On that fateful day, one of the visitors called Kingsley, tricking him into giving them directions to their home.

Mr. Kelvin had already set his plan in motion. He woke up early, drove to Alfonso's home, and honked.

Alfonso stepped out to see who it was.

"Alfonso, we don't have time! Quickly, pack your bags and come with me. Hurry!"

"That I should carry my bags?" Alfonso was confused.

"Please, just do what I'm telling you. I'll explain later."

"Okay."

He hurriedly packed his belongings, left the house, and entered the car without even informing his cousin Kingsley, who was still asleep.

They drove for three hours to the countryside, where Mr. Kelvin took him to a rural home.

"Imagine, you are now safe."

"Safe? I don't get it… From what danger have I been preserved?"

"Recently, Regan's house caught fire. And, unfortunately, the paramedic who arrived with the ambulance to assist him was one of the guests from the party Regan held for you."

"Ooh!" Alfonso was alarmed. "That cannot be! You see my life is a mixture of pain and sorrow."

"Yeah, that is so evident," Kelvin fathomed.

"Just the other day, I was arrested just when I was about to apologise to Regan but imagine what, I never got the chance to apologize."

"Oh, Lord!!" Kelvin marvelled. "And that's how I was sent to prison."

Kelvin's face crumpled.

"That is the most brutal treatment one could ever receive," he affirmed. "It was completely unfair."

"How many months did you stay in prison?"

"Imagine, my other friend is still locked up."

"Oh my?" Kelvin was puzzled by the information.

"We were all sentenced to life imprisonment. It was only because the governor visited and pardoned me that I was set free."

A deep pain ran through Kelvin's heart upon hearing that.

"I'm really sorry."

Oh, and I had forgotten to mention that Kelvin's mother lived alone in the house and had warmly welcomed them.

"What can I serve you, my sons? I'm so delighted with your visit. Being alone at this age is hard, and now the only person I have is the worker," the mother expressed.

"Mom, I'm always here for you! And I'm planning to bring my son over, so don't worry so much."

"Okay." They both laughed.

"That's nice, my son. So, how is Kiambu?"

"Kiambu is fine, and my family is doing well—except for a small problem."

"Oh! What kind of problem?"

"It's my wife." Kelvin slightly paused. "She's in the last stage of cancer." He sighed heavily.

"Cancer?!" She gasped. "Oh, and you never told me… Son," she said, seeming disappointed.

"I just found out she was hospitalized."

"Yeah, and that's pretty much the reason why I've brought this man here. His name is Alfonso."

Alfonso stretched out his hand.

"Oh, how are you?"

"Fine, thank you."

"My son, welcome to my home. It's my pleasure."

"Oh, thanks a lot."

"You see, my wife had a final wish—to be kind to at least two people as a way of remembering her. So, Alfonso, I never knew you had changed. I still perceived you as the cold, brutal murderer. But now, on my wife's request, I had to do what was expected of me. Do you understand?"

Alfonso was overwhelmed. He connected everything.

"I'm so thankful, and surely, nature will repay your kindness."

So, they decided to call one of Kelvin's mates who had conspired against Alfonso.

"Hallo."

"Yes, Mr. Kelvin. I received an emergency, so I had to attend to it. That's why I didn't join you guys... Did you find him?"

The two laughed as he described how they went to their house to no avail. They ended the call and had a period of immense laughter, mocking him.

"They had wished the worst for you. Now, look who is laughing."

Their mom prepared them a late breakfast, which they ate while sharing stories. Alfonso recounted how lucky he had been. He would live to remember that day. What if he were to be rearrested again? How bitter would he have become? What now would be the future's directives? How would he have coped with the news? He really wondered.

"Hey, mommy," Alfonso engaged Mr. Kelvin's mom, "how was your teenagehood?"

"Ah, it was super exciting; let me tell you a story. I used to date a rich guy; he used to give me all the nice gifts, and treated me like a queen but then came that day."

Alfonso became more attentive.

"So, guess what?"

"What!!"

"There is this lady who visited us in the place we were staying and claimed to have been sent by my Fiance's boss. So, this lady puts poison in my man's juice, but what she didn't know is that I had seen and I alerted my man and he swapped the glasses after commanding her to switch on the lights."

The two burst into laughter.

"So, the lady drank the poisoned one; actually, that is how she was admitted. It served as a great lesson to her.

They spent the rest of the day listening to stories surrounding Kelvin's mom's life.

The day ended. They had supper, watched the nine o'clock news, and then retired to bed.

The following day, Kelvin was to visit his longtime village friend, and he invited his other friend to accompany him.

They were on their way to the friend's house when he spotted Geoffrey. He joyfully greeted him, but Geoffrey didn't hear him, so he shouted louder. Geoffrey turned his head... He was wearing tattered clothes and was barefoot.

On seeing him, he ran to him, and upon reaching him, he hugged him and kissed his hand.

"Alfonso, look at how I'm suffering! Life stopped favoring me and my people."

"Oh! Don't say that," Alfonso encouraged him. "See, this life does not favor the faint-hearted. Life is full of frustrations. Look at me, all my family members were murdered, but have I given up? No. So, you, too, should fight on, okay?"

"Alfonso, I'm so much ready. Please give me your number," Geoffrey added. He sighed and explained that after the death of his brother, the house had been seized by the bank due to an overdue loan, and the rest of the family was forced to return to the village since his sister-in-law had no source of income.

Oh, just the explanation itself was painful...

"Don't worry!" Alfonso encouraged him. Deep down, he was saddened. He had recently been uneasy about the people he had murdered and was convinced he had to do something—only then would his pain be minimized.

Immediately, Mr. Kelvin chipped in. "Why don't we follow him to where he lives? Maybe after knowing the place, we can visit some other time."

"Oh... that would be a good idea."

So they went together to Geoffrey's home, sat for a cup of tea, and his family recognized him. They were extremely happy to see him again.

So, they went to Geoffery's home and immediately, Geoffery's sister-in-law approached Alfonso. "I know you from somewhere. Oh, this is our former neighbour."

They hugged each other as both were overjoyed. They had a ten minutes chat as Alfonso mentioned something that made all of them alert.

"I wish to reinstate you guys to your original home but I can't."

Just as he said that, a message popped up on his phone.

"Hello, it's me, Dennis. I came across a video of you yelling simply because you wanted to convey an apology to someone you had wronged but couldn't. It really touched me. I'm glad to announce that, on that basis, it would be diligent of me to return the money I obtained from you... Cheers."

And in that minute, he received a notification on his phone—6.5 million had been deposited.

He stepped aside from them and jumped with all his might! He smiled and experienced intense happiness.

Now that I have the ability, I'll transform and restore their destinies, he thought to himself.

He drew closer to them and gave them the good news.

"I have good news for you." They all turned attentive as Alfonso spoke. "We are all going to Kiambu."

Geoffrey could not believe his ears. He didn't want to doubt, but at the same time, the words were inconceivable.

"What do you mean?" his sister-in-law queried.

"What I mean is that we are going back to the place we used to live! I'll supervise that. In fact, Jeff, put on your sandals because we are headed to the shopping center to buy us some clothes."

Tears rolled down Jeff's face as the thought of being decent once again ran through his mind. He went and formed a circle with his family—two children and the lady—as they began crying uncontrollably while holding each other. Alfonso and Kelvin joined them, and it was the most beautiful sight to behold.

"In fact, we are all going to the shopping center so that all of you can have new clothes."

"Thank you!!!" The lady went and hugged Alfonso, promising that they would do anything to repay him, to which he responded that they didn't have to—he was just fulfilling an obligation.

The others also thanked him from the depths of their hearts.

He asked for a taxi since Geoffrey had the number of one. Alfonso sat in the front seat while the lady, Geoffrey, and the two kids sat in the back.

"You are an amazing man. Seriously, I had a bleak perspective of you, but from this incident, I have just reconsidered everything. Good luck," Mr. Kelvin remarked. He wished to continue with his initial intention of visiting his friend and requested that he come back using the same path they had taken home.

They reached Kerugoya Town, where they first entered a decent hotel and had lunch. Everybody ordered what they wanted, and later, they all had sodas. After that, they visited the largest boutique in Kerugoya, the Kamoronju Enterprises.

"First off, let's choose some appropriate shirts for you, Jeff."

They did so, and he picked about five of them, four trousers, three pairs of socks, and two pairs of shoes. Then it was the lady's turn. She received three dresses, two skirts, a blouse, and a pair of rubber shoes. The kids each received a pair of jeans, a shirt, a jumper, and a pair of sports shoes.

"Are we sorted?"

"I presume so!!!" the lady answered.

They were as happy as larks, and they ended their shopping endeavor as the same taxi awaited them to return home.

Upon their arrival, Alfonso received a call from Kelvin.

"Hey champ, it's all clear. I have spread the message of your kindness to my fellows, and they have been so touched. They said that if you had changed, that was all they could ask for. So, there will be no need to involve the police."

Immediately, Alfonso burst into shouts of joy and could not be contained.

He thanked him so much for taking the initiative to rescue him from the oncoming mayhem and not only that—he had also cleared his name.

"Thank you so much," he expressed.

Amidst all this, Geoffrey's sister-in-law disagreed and screamed at Alfonso.

"All that you are doing is of no use! I detest all this, and I request that you leave now!"

Geoffrey suddenly got heated up and threw a blow at her. He pushed her down and started trampling on her in disdain.

"Don't you ever say such a thing before me again! Are we clear?"

She paused, very frightened, wriggling in pain as she woke up and dusted herself off.

"How could you!! That was unnecessary," she shouted. "He is doing this because of my husband's death! If my husband were here, none of this would be necessary."

Alfonso was shocked beyond words. How could one be so ungrateful? He immediately took off from the scene and headed to his friend's place.

Shortly after Alfonso had left, a message beeped on the lady's phone. By then, she had stopped crying and was seated, contemplating her next move. That's when she opened her phone, and the message she saw drained all her energy.

It was a former neighbor's contemptible message.

"My husband and I just bought a new Mercedes-Benz. Wonder how you are trying to cope with your upcountry life, tihihi."

Immediately, she got so disturbed by the message, especially since the neighbor had posted a picture of the Benz.

What do I do now? Aargh! I only thought that he was doing this for his own self-interest, but now I clearly need that reprieve...

So she was alert to seize any opportunity that would present itself.

The following morning, she pretended to have dialed Alfonso's number by mistake. When he answered, she apologized, but Alfonso challenged her, saying it was okay if she had changed her mind and that she should stop pretending.

They met, with Geoffrey supervising everything, and the five of them left for Kiambu Town.

That day, Kingsley was overjoyed and had waited for his cousin with much eagerness. He was finally happy that he had come, and that's when they went straight to the issue of discussion: how he had escaped another treacherous ordeal.

"Imagine how they appeared!!" Kingsley exclaimed. "They came, like, four of them and were really demanding to have you. I guess you would have just landed in prison once again, but alas… How did it all happen?"

"Yeah, this time, I escaped by a whisker!! Mr. Kelvin knew all that since they were planning with him, and he came very early in the morning and asked me to carry all my belongings and get in his car. He alluded to explaining later, and so that's what I did... I even left you while you were still sleeping. On reaching his upcountry home, he introduced me to his mother, and thereafter, he explained everything. I felt as if I should hug him and tell him how thankful I was. Imagine, he did that out of obligation to fulfill his wife's wish, which was that he was to show kindness to at least two people before she died, and that's just how I was spared."

"Really, there is a God in heaven who watches over His children," Kingsley acknowledged.

So, Alfonso went to the shop he was used to, and by chance, met Karanja.

"Man, I avenged your treatment!!!"

"Treatment?? I don't get you."

"You see, I overheard you on the phone explaining how my uncle had mistreated you by sending you to jail exactly when you wanted to offer him an apology, and it angered me, so I decided to torch his house!"

Alfonso was baffled. "Is that the best move you thought of?"

"What do you mean? I did it out of care and consideration for you."

"That was insensitive!" he claimed as he turned and headed to his home.

That's when he yearned to call Mr. Kelvin and explain everything.

"Now you see the consequences of doing things without proper judgment!!! The guy could have led to the death of his uncle just like that."

"Yes, that's so unfortunate!" he commented.

"Yes, indeed! I do not support it one bit."

"Okay, tomorrow I will visit Mr. Regan and check on him while revealing the truth."

"That's okay. You can tell me if he is not in bad blood with me, then I can visit him..."

"Okay."

Back home, everything was super elegant! The Geoffrey family were the new guests, and they were making themselves comfortable.

Since Alfonso's home was a three-bedroom house, the lady and her kids slept in one bedroom, Kingsley and Geoffrey in the other, and Alfonso in the remaining one. They had to get two extra beds, which Alfonso went to the nearby carpentry shop and bought.

That night, Alfonso was in a frenzy mood and was really enjoying the company of the Geffreys, but after a while, Alfonso sent the kids to the bedroom and told all the others to be attentive, especially Geoffrey and his sister-in-law.

"It has been kind of hard for me because of the secret that I am about to share..."

"Yes, go on," the lady poised.

"So, my earlier life was marked with a lot of recklessness and a don't-care attitude, and I did many regrettable things, including Geoffrey killing your brother."

Geoffrey seemed as if he didn't hear that right. He immediately came out of the house and vanished into the dark.

The lady went and held Alfonso's shirt, tore it apart, and started crying bitterly.

"Where is my husband, you idiot!" She was overwhelmed, and she fell on the ground, still crying, while Alfonso stood there, not knowing how to react.

Two days later, Mr. Kelvin was making a visit to his friend Regan. By that time, he was about to be discharged since he had sustained only minor injuries.

They discussed how he would go about building a new structure once again, but in the meantime, he'd be living with him, which he alluded to.

A week later, Regan had been discharged. Finally, Kelvin sought to tell him the real reason behind his misfortune.

"So, my friend…"

Mr. Regan paid attention to the tone his friend had used.

"Yes?"

"Do you realize that you acted out of ignorance by calling the police on Alfonso?"

Regan was infuriated. "Refrain from mentioning that name! I never want to hear it! Is that okay?"

"Well," Kelvin continued, "but he was in the dark, and he had to give him the truth... Know that, at that time, he had been looking for you to make an apology."

"What do you mean?" Regan's tone changed. "How can you say that?"

"That's the truth. Alfonso is no longer the cold-blooded animal you knew; he has changed."

"Oh, if only that were true."

"Yeah, it is true. Just the other day, he took his neighbors, who were living upcountry, for a whole wardrobe makeover and didn't charge them a cent."

"That's my boy!!" Regan related with how good Alfonso was in the days they were living together and jumped in celebration.

"So he wanted to come and apologize... You mean he is actually sorry??!!!"

"Oh, that springs joy in my heart!! But now he was sentenced to life imprisonment!!!"

"Life imprisonment?" Regan was shocked.

"Luckily, he was pardoned by the governor after a year. And so, when your nephew realized all that—that you sent him to prison exactly when he was coming to apologize—he was infuriated and set your house on fire."

"He will pay dearly!!! My nephew??" Regan was once more shocked.

"He had no heart???" He was disappointed.

Immediately, he called the bank where Karanja had enlisted him as a guarantor.

"Hello, my name is Regan."

"Yes, how can we help you?"

"Oh, I had guaranteed some close relatives a loan, and now he has been unable to repay."

"Oh, give me a minute. His full name, please?"

"Karanja Amigos."

"Oh, so you'd like to pull out from the agreement?"

"Yes, sure!"

"Okay, thank you. I've complied with your request."

The loan was used to buy an acre of farmland, and it was due—more so, late by five months.

Back at Alfonso's house, everything was beginning to fall back into place, and they were, by then, more united. The lady had come to terms with what had happened and was now the person they all loved. It was just awesome.

Some time had passed, and the bank affiliated with Karanja had decided to auction that land to recover the debt. They followed the due process, and soon after Regan heard of the auction, he set himself to participate in it, aiming to be the highest bidder.

Everything went as expected. Immediately, he called Alfonso and made a verbal apology to him, saying that he had a gift to assert his apology. He told him to meet at Thogoto near Gikambura so he could transfer it to him.

Within twenty minutes, Alfonso was there, and the two greeted each other with elated joy.

"How is Alfonso?"

"I'm good and easy."

"Oh, please forgive me for treating you so harshly."

Alfonso remained quiet and looked aside.

"You don't have to be mad, Alfonso. Look at this piece of land. I want to gift it to you as my way of saying sorry."

Alfonso suddenly brightened up.

"Oh, I'm so grateful... Thank you so much, and I'm really sorry for the pain I caused you."

They went ahead and hugged each other in delight. After that, they went to a hotel and had a good time just bonding.

"It is well. I am slowly but surely readjusting to my life's progress," Alfonso stated as they enjoyed their time together.

# Chapter | 5

Definitely Massive!!! Alfonso had gathered four men whom he had appointed to help him navigate his life. Their role was to deal with negativity, whether from people around him or from strangers.

They kept him at home most of the time, but occasionally, they ran errands together.

"This time around, Balito!!! You are now a prominent man," one bodybuilder encouraged him. "Anyone trying to mess with you will be dealt with severely," he added, flexing his muscles.

Alfonso patted him in acknowledgment. "Our job is to ensure that you don't face any negativity at the hands of rogue and callous men," the second bouncer assured.

"Hey, gentlemen, shouldn't we go to the CBD today?" Alfonso suggested.

"Why not? That's a good idea!!" the third one responded.

"We will be as ruthless as possible with anyone who disrespects you," the fourth one added. "From now on, Alfonso should be synonymous with massive respect!"

After having lunch prepared by a newly hired chef, they set off.

It was about an hour's journey by cab (though one of them stayed behind). Upon arriving, they walked for five minutes before reaching a boutique. A stranger took a picture of Alfonso with his bodyguards, seemingly fascinated by them. The team ignored him and continued with their plans.

They entered the first boutique, but Alfonso did not like the clothes there, so they moved to the next one, just a few meters away. The seller was captivated by the sight of the four men.

"Welcome, most prominent citizens," the seller greeted them enthusiastically. "Ah, how are you? What can I offer you?"

"I sell designer suits, shirts, belts, and more. Have a look!"

Alfonso bought some shirts, vests, and trousers, paying directly from his bank account. The seller, excited by the interaction, exclaimed, "You truly command respect!"

The team responded, "Alfonso is synonymous with massive respect!"

Later, they headed to the supermarket, where Alfonso commanded attention. People couldn't stop staring at his well-built bodyguards. At the counter, the cashier looked at Alfonso, smiled, and remarked, "Do you know that you naturally command a lot of respect?"

Alfonso smiled, folded his hands, and bowed slightly, making the moment even more dignified.

That night, only two bouncers stayed behind.

Geoffrey engaged them in a conversation about their profession.

"Well, it's quite fun since we spend most of our time protecting a dignified man. It's actually enjoyable," one of them said, clearly intrigued.

Supper was prepared, and they all feasted together. It was a thrilling experience, spending time with Geoffrey, the bouncers, and Alfonso's family.

Later that night, Kingsley approached his cousin enthusiastically and shouted, "Congratulations!"

"On what, Kingsley?" Alfonso asked joyfully.

"On your newfound status, cousin! You now look like the person you were meant to be."

"Mmmmh!!" Alfonso appeared pleased and thanked him, acknowledging that Kingsley had also played a part in this achievement.

The next morning, after the other two bodyguards arrived, they headed to the piece of land that Regan had gifted Alfonso. Construction was underway, with all workers on-site, diligently going about their business.

As Alfonso walked around the compound, the workers looked at him in amazement.

"Hey, is that our boss?"

"Yeah, I hear so," one worker said as he dropped the brick he had been carrying. At that moment, Alfonso stumbled, but two bouncers were quick to catch him.

"What kind of bad omen is that?" one of them questioned.

"It's nothing significant! It shall be averted," another bouncer reassured.

"Alfonso means respect!" another chimed in.

"Thanks, guys," Alfonso said as he got up. He then noticed the worker and called him over.

"Hey, what's your name?"

"I'm Kilonzo, sir," the young man responded indifferently.

"Oh, that's a nice name! Where are you from?"

"Just around the neighborhood..."

Alfonso nodded and called for the foreman.

"Alfonso commands respect!" the foreman greeted him.

"Thank you so much. Listen, sir, there's this young man, Kilonzo—I want you to triple his pay. Is that okay?"

"Yes, sir! I will implement it right away."

After dismissing the foreman, Alfonso turned to Kilonzo and said, "This house under construction is a gift for someone. I've increased your wage so that you can be the one to deliver the surprise to the rightful owner."

Kilonzo was immediately delighted.

"Sir, may I leave a bit earlier today to open a bank account?"

"Why not? That's in order."

Alfonso instructed one of the guards to inform the foreman to allow Kilonzo to leave early, and the order was promptly carried out.

Alfonso then supervised the construction for a few more hours before leaving.

"Hello!!" Kilonzo made a phone call to the driver of the cab that Alfonso came with.

"Can you give me the directions of the man you carried today from Thogoto?"

"At the construction?"

"Yes, why do you need them?"

"Oh it's something I want delivered and I don't have his number."

"So why don't you get it from the foreman?"

"Sir, I've tried but he is not picking up my phone."

"Okay, he lives at kikuyu-Mai-ihi on the house next to Mai-ihi secondary school with a black gate."

"Thank you so much."

Kilonzo came from a linage of sorcerers and had an issue with Alfonso's flamboyance.

So he connived with a comrade in the same who was to go to Alfonso's house and tell him that he was being summoned by the village elders pertaining a bad omen he had attracted and to get his number.

The next day the guy arose early and headed to Alfonso's house and knocked. Within no time, one bodyguard went for that gate.

"Yes! Who are you and what do you want."

"I am a messenger from the elders of our clan and they have sent me here to invite Alfonso over a bad omen he's attracted."

"Okay, give me a minute."

He went in and told Alfonso of the same as he was overly alerted.

"Okay, let him in."

So the bodyguard went and called him in and as he entered the sitting room, he went slowly and knelt before Alfonso.

*Alfonso is logically equivalent to massive respect* — this accolade had spread all over the city.

"It is well with you, stand up!"

"Master it is with utmost regard for your big name and heightened considerations that I've come to alert you as sent by the elders."

"Continue," he stated as he signalled his bouncers to leave.

"So, as a part of our customs and traditions, it has come to our attention of the possibility of you attracting a bad omen and so the elders invited you to come for a cleansing exercise at our shrine."

"But, how sure am I that this is not a hoax?"

"You show up and clarify for yourself if it is."

"In fact, after the cleansing, the actual cause of unrest will exemplify itself."

"Okay, so which day can I come?"

"Any day from tomorrow."

So the next day, Alfonso woke up early and prepared himself. He took breakfast and after about an hour, he started his journey and since he was requested if he could leave his bouncers, he engaged them in the same and they were just okay. He reached Gikambura within twenty minutes and walked to the place he was directed.

He saw the shrine and on entering it, he was welcomed by Kilonzo and the guy who visited him.

"Oh, welcome Alfonso."

"Yes, I tried my best to arrive in time and so what about the elders? Why is Kilonzo here?"

The guy calmed him and assured him that everything would go as anticipated. So it was about an hour while the guy was making incarnations and that's when he told Alfonso to come near and signalled Kilonzo. Kilonzo came with charm and blew it on Alfonso's face and on that minute, Alfonso lost touch with reality.

Kilonzo jumped in celebration; he made a traditional dance and started watching the man in belittle.

As the other guy now started speaking of his due pay, "Relax, I am paying you; let the charm first take its effect."

He laughed hysterically and could not remove his eyes on Alfonso. All this time, Alfonso started going astray and he wandered out of the house starting to pick leaves and eat them.

He continued like that and didn't recognize a single bit what he was doing and that's when he walked towards Gikambura town and on reaching the town, he removed all his clothes and only remained with his boxers.

At first, people were as shocked as never before; others stared at him in disbelief. Suddenly, he regained consciousness and all that was happening came to his attention. He had been bewitched; he went to a nearby shop and the man ran from him and then he went to another shop, but they also ran. That's when one of the kiosk owners came with a colourful fabric and covered him and he fell on the man and cried and cried and cried. The kiosk owner in turn allowed him to rest and to find comfort. He borrowed him his phone and he called Kingsley.

"Hello, Kingsley, I am in a serious fix, can you send me five thousand, please."

Kingsley became alerted, "What happened? Are you okay?"

"Don't worry, it's really bad..."

"Okay, I am sending the cash."

That's when he returned to the guy and expressed his gratitude, "I am so grateful for your understanding and your empathy." He sighted as tears dropped down his cheeks.

"Now, can I ask you for a favour?"

"Please go ahead."

"Would you go and buy some clothes for me? Specifically a shirt, a trouser, some rubbers and a pair of socks."

"What happened to you? You were walking naked all these while and you did not seem to perceive reality..."

"Don't worry, it's a long story."

"Okay, I am really, really sorry!! Okay I'll be on my way..."

Within no time he had purchased the clothing and he instructed him to go inside the kiosk and change.

"Thank you once more."

He had given him four thousand and kept the remaining one thousand with himself.

Immediately, he headed to the Libyan embassy as from everything that had happened. Libya was the safest country for him to move into as from the stories of heroism in it. He was just fed up with Kenya; from the lifetime imprisonment to his money being swindled at gunpoint to this; he couldn't bear it anymore.

So within no time, he had reached the embassy. He passed through the security after he was frisked and was directed to the main office where he met a secretary dressed in a white suit and black rubbers.

"Hello."

"Hi, too; how can we help you?"

"I have come to apply for permanent residency for your country."

"Oh is that so? Please fill in this document."

"Oh, I will have to go with it and fill it at home; then, I will bring it with my documents attached."

"Okay, no problem."

"Okay, so I'll be there on Thursday by nine am."

So on Thursday, Alfonso woke up early and prepared himself. He took breakfast and after about an hour, he started his journey. He requested if he could leave his bouncers and they were just okay. The visa was processed in time after he was found fit to hold the permanent residence.

That fateful day, Alfonso parked his stuff and was seen to the airport by Kingsley.

He reached at Kenyatta national Airport and he was as happy as a clam.

"Alfonso, we will miss you."

"I will miss you, too."

Within no time, his flight was leaving and he boarded promising to make a phone call to Kingsley after reaching. The flight took thirteen hours and finally he reached Tripoli.

For the past one week, Alfonso spent time in his hotel getting some walks to the town centre and back.

That following week, he had gone to a hotel in the central business district and had ordered a meal when a beautiful lady sat next to him. They both enjoyed their meals, but something unexpected happened. The lady had forgotten her money at home, and upon realizing that, Alfonso offered to pay for her. He paid about twenty-five dinars.

"Oh, thank you so much," the lady expressed in Arabic as she left.

"You are most welcome," he answered, as he was conversant in Arabic since he had learned it from his Arabic-speaking neighbors some years back.

Later that day, he went to a public bench and rested. He sat in solitude, thinking about all the plans he had in Libya and how he was going to execute them. As he sat there, time passed very quickly.

It was dark when Alfonso was woken up by a man.

"Hey, are you okay?"

Alfonso woke up abruptly and realized that it had gotten dark. He had dozed off, and this man was standing in front of him.

"Hey, can I house you? You seem stranded... My name is Ally, and I can tell that things are not going well for you. Am I correct?"

"Well, my name is Alfonso, and I am new to this country..."

"And that's why I am inviting you..."

Alfonso seemed puzzled by the idea.

"Well... I wouldn't mind. In fact, I am kind of bored with the hotel I am currently residing in..."

So they went to nearby apartments, and within twenty minutes, they had arrived.

"Darling, I have a visitor..."

"Oh, darling, welcome."

His wife walked over, kissed him, and took off his coat.

"Hi," she greeted Alfonso after returning to the sitting room.

"So, what's the name of your visitor?"

"Well, my name is Alfonso, Alfonso Balitoa."

"Oh, that's a foreign name, right?"

"Yes, actually, I come from Kenya."

"Oh, Kenya, the pride of Africa..."

"Yes."

"Welcome. So, what do you love about Libya?"

"Oh, I came seeking greener pastures, inspired by the good stories I heard some time ago."

"Oh, and when did you come?"

"About a week ago."

"What stands out to you about our country?"

"I must say you are very friendly, and the cleanliness of your environment is impressive."

All of a sudden, Ally began to vomit. His wife hurriedly went to the bathroom and came back with a basin. All the family members, including the children, were uneasy. They all surrounded him as he complained of severe pain in his lower abdomen.

Alfonso suggested that they take him to the hospital, and his wife agreed. They called a cab and immediately headed to the national hospital. The kids were left with their nanny, who was instructed to wait patiently until they returned.

Within no time, they had arrived. They headed to the reception, where they queued for registration. After a short time, their turn came, and they were asked to pay two hundred dinars before being scheduled to see a specialist.

Soon after, they went in while Alfonso waited outside. The specialist listened to their case, referred them for tests, and asked them to return the day after the following day to collect the results.

That night, they really pondered what the problem could be. They critically analyzed the trail of symptoms but couldn't come to a conclusion.

"I believe we are not in a position to determine the issue. We just have to wait until the day after tomorrow," Alfonso suggested.

"Sure enough, I bet you have a point."

So they all retired to bed, with Alfonso being given a separate room where he laid his head.

The kids were overly concerned and sympathetic toward their dad.

The following day arrived, and everybody was awake.

"Oh, Ally, good morning."

"Morning, Alfonso. Feeling better now?"

"Yes, at least."

"How was your night? How did you sleep?"

"Well, I had some pain initially, but things got better with time."

"Hi, love," Ally's wife greeted from the restroom.

"Hi," he responded as they hugged each other.

"How did you sleep? Did the pain continue?"

"No, honey, it was only there in the initial moments."

"Oh, hi, Alfonso!"

"Hello. How was your night?"

"Quite calm."

"I hope there were no distractions."

"Yes, sure."

"So, I'll be going to town to check for some clothes for you to change into."

"Isn't that awesome? You are so mindful..." Alfonso responded.

"Well, honey, I suppose you should do that now," Ally insisted.

"Hello!" Alfonso greeted one of the kids.

"What happened to Daddy?"

"Daddy is going to be alright, okay? You don't have to worry."

"Okay."

The kid nodded.

"That's better."

"How old are they?"

"Well, that is my second-born, who is ten. My first-born is thirteen, and my last-born is six."

"Well, it seems you planned your family appropriately."

"Yeah, I started my endeavors at the right time."

"As for me, I am celebrating my twenty-eighth birthday this year."

"Oh, wouldn't it be appropriate if you had a child at that age?"

"Yes, sure," Alfonso replied as they all laughed.

The lady returned with a pair of trousers, shirts, sneakers, and socks.

"Here you go."

"Thank you so much. I am delighted."

"You're welcome."

"So, honey, let's go to the sitting room while we wait for Alfonso to take a shower," Aisha suggested.

Alfonso went into the bathroom and freshened up.

Within no time, he had finished. He changed into the new clothes and felt refreshed.

"Can we serve breakfast?"

"Yeah," Ally signaled.

So they ate tea and bread as they continued bonding.

"We are going for the results tomorrow. I hope it's nothing serious," Ally's wife said.

"Yeah, we all hope it's nothing serious. I am still young for all these unpredictable illnesses."

That morning, Ally called in sick at his workplace, and they gave him three days off.

The day went by fast, and Alfonso spent much of his time playing with and answering the kids' questions.

"Sure, they are very curious creatures," he remarked to Alfonso.

In the evening, the pain resurfaced, and they were all terrified. They comforted him as the next day set in.

They woke up as usual, prepared breakfast, and, within a short time, left for the hospital.

They arrived within forty minutes and queued at the reception to present Ally's card. They proceeded to their doctor's office, where they had to wait again. In about ten minutes, their turn came.

They collected the results and handed them over to the doctor.

"Well, you have kidney stones."

Ally and the two others seemed shocked by the results. Ally's wife hugged him while rubbing his back gently. He seemed to doubt the news, but there was nothing he could do.

"This is the worst news I have ever received..." He seemed dejected.

The doctor prescribed some medication, and they left for home.

Immediately after they arrived, Alfonso decided to take his leave, thanking them for their generosity and kindness.

About a week later, Alfonso received a call from Ally's wife.

"Hey, how are you?"

"I'm doing just fine."

"Oh, things have gotten really worse..."

"Why do you say that?"

"My husband's kidney has failed, and he has been admitted."

"Oh no! I must come to visit him."

"Okay, that's not the major problem. He needs a kidney from someone..."

"Oh, I'm really shocked by this news."

"So, when are the visiting hours?"

She explained and told him that Ally was in Ward Eight.

Without wasting time, Alfonso got ready and headed to the hospital. He was early by forty minutes, planning to arrive just as the visiting hours started.

He was right on time and went directly to his bed.

"Hallo..."

"Oh, my good friend, surely may the heavens bless you."

"Thank you, Ally. How is the situation?"

"Well, I was admitted, and upon further investigation, both my kidneys were found to be damaged."

"Oh, wouldn't you be happy if I were to help you?"

"Help? How?"

"I am willing to donate one of my kidneys to you."

He looked him straight in the eyes to see if he was joking, but Alfonso smiled and held his hand.

"I am sure of what I am saying."

That's when Ally burst into uncontrollable tears, overwhelmed by the issues of dialysis and the aftermath of his condition.

"I highly appreciate your sacrifice. You have saved my life..."

So Ally talked to his doctor about the matter, and they scheduled the surgery for the next two weeks.

Ally's wife came to visit him.

"Honey, I've received a donor for my kidney!"

She immediately kissed him in a moment of happiness.

"Guess who it is?"

"Who, honey? Tell me!" Aisha asked curiously.

"Alfonso."

"What?! I knew he was such a sweetheart."

She was touched, and she began to shed tears.

"Honey! This is the best news I've heard!"

They hugged, feeling grateful.

Time went by fast, and finally, the moment Ally had been waiting for arrived.

That day, Alfonso arrived at the hospital at around ten and went directly to where he had been instructed. The surgery took three hours, and they were done. Ally followed, and his surgery also took three hours.

Afterward, Ally was taken back to the ward.

# Chapter| 6

It was a dark, chilly night, and the breeze seemed to sing to the tune of the heart.

"I am very lucky. In this country, I maximize my chances."

Immediately, the lady whom he had paid the bill for passed by and smiled as soon as she saw him. But Alfonso maintained a serious demeanor.

The lady, convinced enough, went to the hotel where they had met and requested to talk to the waiter who had served him.

"Man, you can't believe whom I saw," she said joyfully.

"Seriously... you mean you have seen something worthwhile?" he answered.

"From how you're behaving, it's something great."

(She was a loyal customer, and they had formed a friendship.)

"Yeah! I saw the same man who paid my bill the other day, and my, oh my, he is handsome. Jeeez!"

"Someone is in love! Someone is in love! So why didn't you talk to him last time?"

"Oh, I was still contemplating going back to my boyfriend, but as it turns out, he doesn't deserve me. So I want you to help me out."

"Okay, what can I do for you?"

"I want you to trace where he lives."

"But that is close to impossible. Please don't put me in such a fix."

"But who is going to help me if not you?"

"So what do you suggest I do?"

"Okay, here's the deal. The next time he comes here to eat, I want you to inform my stuntman so that he can be here as soon as possible. Then, he will follow him secretly. Is that okay?"

"Yes, that's workable."

The next day, Alfonso visited the hotel, and as usual, he was served his meal. Then, the waiter immediately called the stuntman the lady had instructed, who lived nearby.

Within seven minutes, he arrived at the hotel. He went straight to the waiter, who secretly pointed at Alfonso.

"So, there's the man..."

"Cheers, we'll know how to proceed from here," he said as he left the hotel.

Alfonso finished his meal, paid, and stepped out of the hotel.

They were two—the first man and his accomplice. They let Alfonso walk about two hundred meters before they started the car and followed him. It was too vague to notice since other cars were passing by.

They followed him until he entered New Tripoli Hotel and immediately called Amina.

"Hello, boss, we've got his location. He is currently staying at New Tripoli Hotel."

"Okay, well done."

"Anything else you might need from us?"

"No, I will communicate the next plan when we meet."

So Amina devised a plan: The two men would kidnap Alfonso, and then she would rescue him to seem like the good guy.

That is what she communicated to her two stuntmen.

It was a chilly afternoon when Alfonso came out of the hotel he was staying in. He wanted to take a stroll to the town center when, after walking for a while.

A black car drove past and suddenly stopped and its doors opened abruptly as a man stepped out and forcefully grabbed him.

The car door abruptly opened as a man stepped out and forcefully grabbed him.

"Help! Help!"

He tried to shout for help, but they were too quick.

"Identify yourself."

Alfonso tried, but to no avail.

The car sped off, leaving people in shock.

"Identify yourself."

The guy sitting at the back pulled out a gun and pointed it at Alfonso.

"Keep nagging me, and I promise you won't make it to the next junction."

Alfonso, intimidated, kept quiet.

They drove for about fifty minutes and arrived at a residential area. They entered a plot with other tenants and instructed Alfonso,

"Take the steps and follow us. Any small mess will cost you."

They entered the fourth floor, door number five. They had been there for about an hour and a half when there was a knock at the door. One of them opened it, and a man requested to speak with him outside for a few minutes.

As all this was happening, Alfonso heard Amina's voice downstairs. Immediately, the second man stepped outside, and as they had planned, the two police officers pulled out their pistols and ordered them to kneel.

One of the officers immediately entered as Alfonso gasped for air.

"Sir, it is well!"

"What do you mean?"

"We are police officers."

"Huh!"

Alfonso felt immense relief.

"Sir, I don't know what plans they had for me. Being new to this country, I didn't know what to expect."

"Don't worry. You are now free. Your savior is down there..."

He looked down only to see Amina waving at him with a smile.

"You mean it was you?" he thought to himself.

They walked down the staircase while the two kidnappers were handcuffed.

Alfonso was relieved. Amina explained that she was at the scene and couldn't just watch such an atrocity slide.

"Oh! You have saved me. I am so glad. Thank you."

Alfonso said it more as a formality.

"We are heading for another assignment, so you won't get the chance to write a statement, but I expect your friend to come later and write it on your behalf."

"Okay, no problem," Alfonso responded.

"So, can I know the name of my savior?"

"Oh, he's so sweet," Amina thought to herself.

"My name is Amina. Remember at the hotel when you paid my bill because I had forgotten my money?"

"Yes, I remember you. This is truly a coincidence. So I helped you, and now you've helped me—what a desirable connection."

"So, what had they planned to do to you?"

"These incidents are very frightening. I was just filled with anxiety."

They walked to the nearby bus station.

"Would you like to visit my home?"

"Listen carefully. Don't mistake my words for foolishness. I am a rogue man when need be... okay? You think I don't know you were responsible for what just happened?"

Alfonso was just pretending.

"What?!"

Amina was filled with embarrassment and fear. She covered her mouth in shock, wondering what kind of man Alfonso was.

"This world is crazy," he thought to himself.

Amina felt ashamed. She retreated to her father's home in the suburbs, unable to escape the disgust she felt toward herself.

"How could I be so evil? What came over me?! Ugh! I thought it would end in my favor... I was too blinded."

Just then, the man from the hotel called.

"Hey, I need my money..."

By the time the third week arrived, Alfonso had moved into Ally's apartment and had started living there. He had also started a small electronics business, which was thriving.

One day, Ally's wife was passing by when she overheard Alfonso talking with Kingsley on the phone.

"Maaan! Am I hearing things right?" Kingsley was flabbergasted, "is this the best cousin! Oh Alfonso I really had waited for this call,"

"Yes, Kingsley, man, I am telling you I am in luck imagine. I spent only a week at the hotel and was adopted by a new family."

"Wow that's immense luck!" Kingsley responded.

"And not only that but they even opened an electronics shop for me."

The chat lasted for minutes.

"Actually, I have never healed from the pain of having my father killed," Alfonso sighed.

Kingsley immediately brought up the notion that there was a good reason for that and that Alfonso should focus on changing what he could and leave what he couldn't to fate.

"You have a good chance right now. Do your best, and I'm sure the universe will repay you."

"Thanks, cousin, for those words of encouragement. I'll be attending to customers now."

"Okay, we'll talk later. Ciao."

"Alfonso..."

"Yes, Aisha?"

"Did you lose your father?"

Alfonso was overwhelmed with emotions and had a flashback of that fateful day.

"I was returning home from school—back then, I was in my final year of my second degree in engineering—when I heard gunshots from a distance. I was greatly perturbed, and my instincts told me to go home. When I arrived, I found all my family members dead."

Aisha's eyes focused as she tried to get a mental picture of the incident. At that moment, the most desirable version of Alfonso was registered in her mind. She saw him as a very humble and pure soul.

Immediately, Aisha excused herself, went aside, booked a flight to Kenya and returned. She was determined to know Alfonso's full background.

"So, where did you use to live?"

"Oh, why are you asking?"

"I'll be visiting your home country in three days, and I might make a stop there."

"Oh, my hometown is Kiambu, in a place called Mai-Ihi."

"Would you mind giving me the number of a familiar friend or relative?"

"Oh, here you go." He handed her Kingsley's number. "That's my cousin, Kingsley."

"Okay, glad to have it. Goodbye."

Aisha arrived home and began preparing for her trip. She called her husband and explained her need to visit Kenya.

Meanwhile, Amina had found some relief and was now stable. She had returned home and was relaxing when her phone rang.

"Hey! Listen carefully. You are going to pay me five times what you owe me!"

"And who made you believe that lie?"

It was one of the hired goons.

"Well, you have no options. My marriage cannot end simply because I provided my services. My wife's friend was among the neighbors, and she witnessed me taking the man you ordered us to kidnap. She reported everything to my wife. Now, my wife is threatening to leave me. If you were concerned enough, you'd increase my pay."

She had not paid them yet.

"At least that way, I can buy something nice for her to make her stay. So, I want nothing less than fifteen thousand dinars. Are we clear?"

"Come out of your delusions! Furthermore, I never succeeded in what I had planned, which means your work was futile."

"Whether you convinced him or not is none of my business. All I want is my money."

"Same case for me. Whether your wife stays or not is none of my business."

So, she paid them a sum of three thousand dinars each.

Night had fallen, and her father was calling her.

"Hello! I have toiled all my years to give you an education and everything else you needed in life, and this is what I get?"

"What is it, Daddy? You have provided for me, and I am grateful."

"Which phase of your psychosis prevented you from collecting your brother?"

That's when it clicked in her mind—she had been reminded to pick up her little brother from boarding school as they were closing that day.

"Do you understand the mess you've put me in?" her father reprimanded. "Your little brother is now lying in the hospital with serious injuries because you couldn't follow simple instructions."

A wave of bitterness washed over her, and to make matters worse, her father forbade her from ever setting foot at their home. He also said he did not expect her to visit her younger brother in the hospital.

She pulled her hair in dismay, feeling like the most useless person on earth. Oh, how she loved her little brother!

"How could I have forgotten something so important?" she reproached herself.

Just then, a message notification popped up.

The message read: Dear customer, a debit of one hundred thousand dinars has been made from your account.

"Oh no! This can't be true! No!"

Someone had just stolen her money! Tears trickled down her cheeks as she fell to the floor, yelling loudly.

"This can't be! This can't be!"

She rolled on the floor helplessly—she had never experienced such a devastating moment.

Later, she went to a shop when a fast-approaching vehicle forced her to hurry to a safe zone. In a split second, everything happening in her life caught up with her, and she experienced a panic attack. She collapsed onto the ground.

The car that was approaching braked suddenly, but a truck behind it collided with it, pushing it forward until it reached where Aisha lay, making an impact.

The entire place came to a standstill. Both drivers got out of their vehicles. The first driver, furious, turned to the other.

"You imbecile!" he shouted. He moved toward the other driver, looking as if he was about to throw a punch when pedestrians intervened, trying to calm him down.

"Look, it's not his fault," one of them said.

"You are an inconsiderate man!" the second driver retorted.

"How can you start blaming people while there is a casualty lying on the ground?"

The first driver came to his senses. "Oh, forgive me. It's just that my car is new, and I was consumed by rage..."

"Look, she seems very injured," the first driver signaled.

"Yes! We need to take her to the hospital urgently. Hurry, we can put her in my vehicle."

Two witnesses joined them, and they rushed to the hospital.

They arrived at the national hospital and took Aisha to the casualty area.

As they scrolled through her phone, searching for someone to contact, they found her father's number and called him.

"Hello, this is a well-wisher calling from the national hospital."

"Is anything the matter?"

"Yes, we just had an accident, and your daughter was slightly injured."

Frequencies of shock registered all over his body as he began to breathe heavily. "Honey, hurry! Take Junior to our neighbors and ask them to watch him for us... there's an emergency concerning our daughter, and we can't afford to delay."

"No, Amina!"

"Please, this is not the time for questions... do as I have told you."

"Oh no, this can't be happening! Junior, come, baby. Please tell me you'll be a good boy, okay?"

"Mommy, where are you going?"

"I'll tell you later, okay, swee—"

"Okay, Mom."

They went to the neighbors, who gladly accepted to watch over him.

It took about fifty minutes to reach the hospital, and the two ran hastily into the casualty area.

"Sweetheart, oh no... Sweetheart... you are stronger than this! You need to fight! Fight for us! Fight for your brothers. Fight for everyone."

She was weak and couldn't talk.

The next day, Alfonso was admitted due to pain in his lower abdomen. The pain was so intense that he had to be admitted, and they placed him in the bed next to Amina.

Alfonso woke up and saw the hips of a lady next to him (she was facing the other side), so he decided to call her. She responded, turning her head—yes—and immediately, their eyes locked. Alfonso had never seen such beauty. Yes, they had been together, but he had not seen this version—the fragile, cute Amina.

"Alfonso."

And in that moment, it dawned on Amina that what she was feeling was the reason for everything. Because she just felt a sharp sense of peace from her head to her toes, and her mind cleared all of a sudden. It was as if she had gotten a six-figure salary.

"Yes, my dear."

"Oh, I have missed you. I couldn't stop thinking about you."

"Really?"

"Yeeess..."

Oh, it was as if the universe was orchestrating a love function for them. Alfonso had never been in love, but what he was feeling was a sure bet.

"I am sorry for being rude to you the last time we met."

"Oh, and I'm sorry for all that you endured under the rogue men. It was unnecessary. Honestly, you are the love of my life."

Oh, what a good feeling it was hearing those words come out of a beautiful lady.

"As for me, even the first time that I met you at the hotel was a wholesome moment, and I wasn't sure whether to follow my heart or not. That's why you smiled at me later, and I never smiled back."

It was nighttime, and visitors were not allowed in the hospital. Morning came, and Amina's parents finally arrived and found her awake. Oh, her dad went and hugged her as her mom joined them.

"Oh, honey, we were so worried."

"Yes, Dad. I was told I collapsed in the middle of the road."

"Honey, don't worry. At least you are alive."

"Okay... I was really worn out by the events happening in my life, and I guess that's why I passed out."

"Oh, don't worry."

At the same time, Ally and his wife came, and as soon as Alfonso saw them, he felt a sigh of relief.

"Alfonso..."

"Yes!! So it means that I matter to you guys..." He was overexcited, and they all gave him that look. "Aha, just kidding."

"Of course you matter! Without you, my husband could never have made it, and probably the reason you are here is because of that transplant..."

There was an error in the hospital system, as Alfonso was supposed to be taken to the ward but ended up in the casualty section.

"Oh, I am delighted..."

Within two days, both were discharged, and the first thing they did after meeting up was cuddle. They spent the whole day together at Alfonso's house and simply couldn't get enough of each other. To Alfonso, that was a new experience.

"Honey, you see these people who look innocent? Oh! Don't be fooled. These are people with very dark associations."

"What do you mean?"

"Well, not everyone you see here on the streets is clean. Some districts in Libya are known for their involvement in black magic. Look at a guy like Hassan—he is the Minister of Trade in Libya, but rumor has it that he consults mediums, and that's his source of power."

"So, honey, you better be cautious."

"Okay, I get it."

Alfonso decided to check out the man his girlfriend had mentioned on social media, and some kind of magnetic wave came over him. It was as if he had been opened up to a portal in the spiritual realm, and what followed was an epiphany.

His woman came out naked, as that was the required appanage, and after fifteen minutes of sex, Alfonso had it clear in his mind that he was going to join politics. Ah, and all this was dependent on the vibe he got whenever he looked at the minister.

The day was finally here, and Aisha was on her way to Kenya. She left early at eight and was on her way to Tripoli International Airport. In an hour, she was there. Her plane was scheduled for eleven a.m., and she waited at the bay.

Eleven arrived, and her flight was announced. She hurried and boarded it. She was all excited about going to Kenya for the first time, and all the passengers looked bright.

"Welcome to Turkish Airlines... We are about to take off."

Aisha was as excited as a kid at Christmas. She was finally going to familiarize herself with the background of one of the greatest men in her life—Alfonso.

During the journey, she pondered on how it would feel when she finally met Kingsley. Oh, what a convincing course.

It took about thirteen hours and fifteen minutes to finally reach Nairobi, where they landed at Jomo Kenyatta International Airport.

She was wowed! The place looked stunning. Oh!!! She couldn't take enough pictures.

"I wish I had visited this place earlier. It's pretty much evident it will be worth it. I'll get to go to Alfonso's roots, the place where he grew up, the people he interacted with, and I'll be immersed in his culture. Oh, I have never seen a man like Alfonso. He is kind, fun to be around, and has endured so much pain. Aha!"

So, Kingsley had arranged a taxi for her. She called the driver and boarded it.

"Are you Mrs. Aisha?"

"Yes. And are you Mr. Bill?"

"Yes. Oh, welcome to Kenya."

"Thank you very much. I suppose you know where I'm headed to, right?"

"Sure, that will take thirty minutes."

"No worries."

So, they embarked on the journey as Bill gave her some background information about the places they passed through.

Eventually, they arrived, but now the driver demanded double the fare Kingsley had cited as the due price.

"But according to what we had agreed on, I owe you a thousand, not more. If you demand extra, then you will have to talk to my host," she alluded.

"My friend, you are paying me two thousand."

(Aisha had gotten Kenyan currency at the local bank.)

They had gotten loud when a stranger noticed and approached.

"Are you guys okay?"

"Imagine, I have just landed, and now he wants to overcharge me..."

"Is that true?" the man enquired.

"No, I had spoken with the cousin, and I told him that I'd be charging two thousand."

"Well, the solution to this is easy... Can you give me the number of your cousin?"

So, he dialed and gave Aisha the phone to tell him what had happened and that she was waiting for him to come.

"Wow!!!!!!! Kingsley!!!!"

He was here and was mesmerized by the fact that the stranger was Moses, one of Alfonso's former bouncers.

He went ahead and did a dance as both of them celebrated the reunion.

All this time, Aisha was intrigued by the fact that the situation had turned positive, with the stressor turning into happiness.

"Where is Alfonso? Oh, the boss for whom respect was his second language!!"

"Surely??"

On hearing that, Aisha seemed puzzled.

Immediately, Aisha conceptualized an idea.

So, Kingsley sought to solve the problem with the driver, and they agreed that he was to be paid one thousand five hundred for taking them to Mai-Ihi, where Kingsley's home was located.

Within twenty minutes, all four had arrived.

Aisha decided that she was going to talk with her rich uncle to lend Kingsley some money and bring the guy who had called Kingsley to Libya.

Within the course of that week, they shared the history of Alfonso as she interacted with the Geoffreys. She was overexcited to hear how Alfonso had rescued them from their village and was now even building a house for them. That gave her more determination to continue deliberately working for Alfonso's well-being.

At the end of her visit, she oversaw the process of getting a visa allocation for Moses.

# Chapter | 7

It was the following week, and Moses had gotten the full account of what had happened to his boss. Kilonzo was wandering around Kikuyu when he saw Moses from a short distance ahead. He tried to hide but then decided there was no need. That was when the other guy that Moses was walking with (still one of Alfonso's bouncers) received a phone call from someone who seemed to be Alfonso. According to their conversation, Alfonso would be running for a top seat in the Libyan government, and at that moment, immense shame befell Kilonzo.

"Oh, do you remember what happened to you under the construction guy?" the man asked.

"Yes, that's in the past. I decided not to seek revenge even though that had been the highest form of disgrace."

Kilonzo's conscience broke to the last chunk, and he immediately went home.

Over the next three days, an illness began tearing him apart. Worse still, his friend had turned against him.

His days started with him immersed in tears and ended the same way. His mother was less bothered as this had been a long time coming. She only brought food for him, fed him, and when he was unable to eat, she left with a heavy heart.

His friends came to visit him one by one. They pitied him and kept him company, but many cringed at his excruciating pain. His skin developed sores from head to toe, and he couldn't even turn to the other side without feeling immense pain.

That was when Moses heard the news and decided to pay him a visit.

He came with one other bouncer, and though it took time, Kilonzo recognized them.

"My friends," he said.

"Yes," they responded.

"Don't pity me. I am paying for my deeds."

"Why do you say so?"

"I bewitched Alfonso after perceiving that he would be great and thus wanted to hinder him. I made him remove all his clothes..." Before he could finish, Moses turned aside under the weight of the revelation. His friend pressed his eyes with his right hand, fighting back tears.

"But now I am the victim of my own actions. I overheard you speak to him and was really perturbed by the news that he is now in a foreign country chasing his dreams... Well..."

By now, he was very weak. He coughed loudly, his breathing became heavier, and all the people came out of the house (he was lying on a mat outside).

Before he died, he said that Alfonso would surely succeed in his endeavors as a politician in the foreign land since he had an insight into how the spiritual realm operates. And since he had conquered all that was sent his way to hinder him, he would surely succeed. He breathed his last as his mother covered his body.

"I know you were innocent. I know you deserved none of this! I am the one to blame!" A feeling of sadness engulfed the mother as she was unable to bear it. "I did not raise him in the right statutes..." she regretted as the sisters, too, were overwhelmed, and they all comforted each other.

"Mommy, you did your best. Don't cry..."

The visa was approved, and Moses was on his way to join Alfonso, courtesy of Aisha. He was overexcited to be boarding the plane. He was certain that he was fulfilling his purpose through Alfonso, and he couldn't wait to play his part in making Alfonso great.

As usual, the flight took thirteen hours and fifteen minutes and landed at Tripoli International Airport.

On looking out, he saw Alfonso and another girl. The best feeling ever surged through Moses. He ran to him and hugged him.

"How are you, my friend!? Alfonso, my man!!"

The two were overjoyed as Alfonso saluted him for the excellent work he had done back in Kenya. He assured Moses that he would now be instrumental as Aisha had signaled to him.

"Oh, meet my girlfriend, Amina."

"Amina, this is Moses," Alfonso said.

"Moses, this is Amina."

"Pleasure to meet you."

"Pleasure to meet you, too."

They connected as Moses expressed his delight.

They first went to the shops, ordered some snacks, and boarded a cab to Alfonso's place, where they cooked a late lunch and feasted.

"I already have a place rented for you," Alfonso said.

"Wait, before we leave, what's that phrase you used?"

"Which phrase?"

"The one you used with Kingsley." (Moses had hailed him to Kingsley during her stay in Kenya.)

"Alfonso is logically equivalent to massive respect..."

Everyone was happy as the hailing lightened up the mood.

They dispersed as Aisha took Moses to her house and later to the apartment where he would stay.

"So the main reason I've brought you here is: one, yes, you know I understand that your friend is a very special person and has contributed significantly to our lives..."

"Who? You mean Alfonso? Oh, yes!!"

"I can't express enough how true that is... You see, in Kenya, he was the most cherished individual..."

Aisha rejuvenated as she asserted that Moses was expected to spread Alfonso's fame, to which he gladly agreed.

With him, he had carried a gratitude letter from Geoffrey, which read:

TO ALFONSO BALITOA (my greatest friend),

It is with profound joy that I write this letter, acknowledging your kindness and consideration as exemplified by your participation in my family's affairs and your concern for our future. I will never forget the day you replaced my tattered clothes with new ones and covered my feet with fashionable shoes—not only for me but for my whole family. And then you took us from our village home, and now the house that you promised is still under construction. Thank you so much... We will be forever indebted to you!

Regards,

Moses met with Aisha that morning and expressed his desire to carry out some activities, so she granted him seven hundred dinars, and he was off.

Later that day, Alfonso left for the registrar of political parties. He first approached the secretary, who scheduled him to meet the registrar in two hours. Within no time, the door opened, and he entered.

"Hello, sir."

"Yes, hello. How can I help you?"

"Well, my name is Alfonso Balitoa, and I came to inquire because I felt challenged..."

"Yes, continue."

"Honestly, I am a foreigner and wanted to contribute to the growth of this country..."

"How old are you?"

"I am 28."

"I'm sorry, but you aren't eligible! The constitution states that only individuals aged thirty-five and above can be elected, and no foreigners can run for that seat."

Alfonso recoiled at the stipulations and sighed heavily. "It seems luck is not on my side." He excused himself.

Moses was familiarizing himself with the city when he passed by the office of the registrar. He mistakenly dropped the letter as he drew his handkerchief and left. Later, a stranger picked it up, unfolded it, read it, and then dropped it.

Time had elapsed, and the registrar was heading home when he suddenly spotted the letter. He read through it.

"This man went all this way to prove to me that he is a good man. Why can't people mature up and stick to their path?" he wondered.

He threw the letter, but before doing so, he snapped a picture of it—just in case it was genuine.

Alfonso was despondent while returning home, but on the way, he met Moses.

"Alfonso is logically equivalent to massive respect..."

He afforded a smile.

They deliberated on the issue, and Moses spiked his moods. "Everything will go on as expected. Don't worry…"

Later that day, the registrar received a call from the Permanent Secretary.

"Hello."

"I'm fine…"

"Well, Mr. Ahamed, I'm sorry for this, but you are fired. Your conduct has been found wanting. So, all the changes will be effected, including the repossession of the cars allocated to you and any other privileges."

His mind went blank.

"Sir, you cannot do this to me," he tried to credit himself with all manner of soothing words… but the phone call ended.

The following morning, a new registrar had replaced the outgoing one. He arrived at about eight a.m. and greeted the secretary.

"Hallo, beautiful. Sorry, do I know you?"

Mustapha had just reported to work.

"Ummm… would you like to know me?"

"Let me see do you love ice cream?"

"Yes! Oh so that's the path you've taken."

"Yes, I have to know whether we are compatible."

"Okaaay."

"So which flavour do you like most? Strawberry, vanilla or chocolate?"

"I prefer vanilla!"

"Just like me; ooh, now I would like to know you."

The two bonded as Mustapha made him aware that he was the new registrar and she was more than happy at the news and afterwards Fiona was to bring him up to speed with the activities that had happened before.

As he was waiting to be presented with the ongoing work, he decided to go over the CCTV footage. He was about to end the exercise when he saw the former registrar picking up the letter. He had clearly seen that it was dropped by a passerby (Moses). He read the contents of the letter through the CCTV and had also watched from the secretary's CCTV that a man by the name Alfonso—the same name in the letter—had come for some inquiry. At first, he thought that maybe it was manipulation by Alfonso, but when he reviewed the other footage, he ruled that out, considering the innocence of the man who had dropped it.

He read the letter and was wowed by the kindness of Alfonso. He told himself that he had to do all he could to make sure Alfonso got whatever he was looking for at the office.

Phone call…

"Hello."

"Hi, who is this?"

"Oh, my name is Mustapha, and I'm the new registrar of political parties. Were you helped yesterday?"

"Sir, we can't discuss this over the phone. Can I come over and have this conversation in person?"

"Okay, so I'll be there at two."

"Okay, glad! I'll be waiting."

Alfonso jumped with happiness as he called his woman, who was happy too.

"Could this mean that we are to be considered?"

"Yes! That's its implication. Our prayers have been answered…"

"Yeeeeaaa!!"

"You can say that again…"

He called Aisha, who directed him to start formulating his political party since he carried favor, and she predicted that the new registrar would instigate a move to amend the constitution just to suit his endeavors.

"Oh, you think so?"

"Yes, I don't think—I'm certain."

Oh! Alfonso fancied up…

At about two, Alfonso was already at the office. He talked to the secretary regarding the issue and was allowed in. He went there as meek as a lamb.

"Oh, hi. How are you?"

"I'm fine, sir. So, what brought you here yesterday?"

"Sir, I was really hoping to register a political party when the former registrar alluded that I cannot run for office since I'm twenty-eight years old and a foreigner."

"Okay," the man was intrigued. "So, which seat do you want to occupy?"

"Sir, I want to run for president in the next elections."

"You have all the leverage you desire," he thought to himself as he requested Alfonso to go home, assuring him that he would give him a call to inform him about the developments enforced.

"Okay?"

"Okay, sir."

He left the office, and the registrar retrieved the letter, which he had taken a picture of, and read it once more.

"This is the kind of man we need in this country…"

Immediately, he called his friend, the MP for Benghazi District, and expressed the need to see him. They scheduled a meeting for the afternoon of the next day. True to his word, he arrived with his escort, as his security guard opened the door. He alighted and went straight to the office as the registrar welcomed him.

"Mr. Mustapha…"

"Yes, Mr. Khaled."

"Oh, so delighted to have you. Imagine having a person like this at the topmost position in our country?"

He retrieved the photo from his phone and gave it to Khaled to read.

"Wow! Wow! Wow! Who is this person?" Khaled asked as he paused for a moment and reflected on the brightness of the future the country would have if everything went as expected for Alfonso.

"But the problem is, he is a foreigner and only twenty-eight years old…"

"That's not a problem because what else are we paid for if not for intervening in such times? Don't worry. I'll submit a proposal to the legislative council so that it can be brought to the National Assembly and the Senate. With that, let's have a positive outlook."

So, he did as he had suggested, and the bill was tabled in the house. It went through the first, second, and third readings, and the majority of MPs voted for it. The same case applied to the Senate. Finally, it was passed into law that the minimum age for being a president was twenty-seven years and that any foreigner could become president, provided his record was clean.

"Alfonso is logically equivalent to massive respect," Amina encouraged her husband.

"Baby… now you have everything it takes to be whatever you want, okay?"

"Whatever I want?"

"Yes, hunny… whatever you want."

"What if all I want is to become your husband?"

Amina brightened and hugged him.

"You are so sweet!!"

"You can say that again…"

"Come here." She drew closer as he kissed her fervently.

Alfonso called all his acquaintances for a meeting, and all came, including Ally, Aisha, Moses, and his girlfriend.

They started by thanking their Maker since He had been so good to them—from the day Alfonso's parents were murdered to his release from prison. They asked Him for guidance and that He would direct his ascendance to power, enabling him to become president. They acknowledged that it would take divine intervention since he had no political party yet; he required one to be elected as president.

They sighed as they concluded the prayer.

"Guys… we need to discuss various issues. I have three agendas for our discussion.

The first one: money for the campaign. The second one: formation of a political party and how to go about it.

The third one: how to mobilize political rallies."

"We don't need a lot of money for the campaign," Aisha postulated.

"Approximately how much is needed in your country?"

"A lot, very much. You have to give each supporter something like three thousand Kenyan shillings, and you know those rallies are attended by tens of thousands of people. We have around twenty rallies throughout the campaign. So that would total about one billion Kenyan shillings."

"I've heard of such countries, but our case is different. Here, there's nothing like bribing—it's your policies that get you into office. So, you'll need a shredded version of that. With something like two million dinars, you're good to go."

He seemed doubtful at first, but then his face filled with relief.

"That is so manageable!!! What if it was in your country!?"

Aisha joked, and they all laughed.

"Will you stop with your petty jokes?" Alfonso commented.

"My uncle is a rich man and I can talk to him regarding your state."

"Oh my God!!!" Alfonso began crying as Aisha gave him a warm hug, "it's okay."

"You donated your kidney; this is my turn to help you, okay?"

"Okay, Aisha, I am so grateful."

She smiled.

"You are always welcome," Aisha continued, "I'll talk to my uncle and he will give me not less than two million dinar."

Alfonso warmly hugged her again.

"Oh, I'm so grateful."

She smiled.

"You are always welcome. I'll talk to my uncle, and he will give you not less than two million dinars..."

"Yes!!!!" Alfonso celebrated as others clapped for Aisha.

"And just like that, we're sorted..." Moses noted.

"Alfonso is logically equivalent to massive respect!" Aisha hailed.

The third agenda was mobilization of political rallies and Moses read it. There was intense silence and Alfonso abruptly smiled at Moses who was shocked.

"Alfonso, what's up? You know why I am smiling?"

"Oh, I don't."

"You are the best person for that job" and everybody was elated in support of Alfonso. Moses joined them as he laughed noting how Alfonso was chicky and he agreed on the role.

"Thank you, Moses," Alfonso revered, "Your efforts will definitely payoff."

"Sure, Alfonso. Of all people, for your sake, I am more than willing to do it."

So Moses concluded the meeting as he hailed Alfonso, who was logically equivalent to massive respect, and everyone revered him.

"So guys, there is tea and some snacks for you. Make sure you enjoy yourselves, and thank you so much for your attendance."

Alfonso and Amina met in the kitchen, savoring the moment.

"Come here, you cutie pie."

"Oh baby, I was dying when people were conveying their reverence."

They kissed for about five minutes straight.

"It's okay, Hun. Let's meet after everyone has left."

They took their tea, and within twenty minutes, everyone had left. Aisha agreed with the boss, and they planned to meet his millionaire uncle that Saturday, as she would talk to him about the donation.

Saturday arrived, and the millionaire showed interest in Alfonso after realizing how respectable he was.

They left their apartment at about ten a.m. and traveled to Zawiya, which took about fifty minutes.

Aisha ran upon seeing her uncle as they hugged fervently.

"It's been so long and I've really missed you."

"Yes, Aisha; I had dreaded for this day."

Alfonso had, by then, approached and he bowed.

"This is the man I was telling you earlier about."

"Wow, the man is so well-mannered." Faris thought to himself.

"Yes, uncle, meet Alfonso and Alfonso, meet my uncle Faris."

"Oh, I'm so honoured," Alfonso exclaimed and the three had a very good time together and Faris had the verification he needed for supporting him.

The millionaire found that urgency in Alfonso and decided he would invest in him.

Immediately, Alfonso received a call from Geoffrey, who was overly happy, stating that the house he was building for them was nearly complete. Alfonso gave him hope, assuring him that his promise would hold ground.

Aisha's uncle overheard the conversation and smiled to himself, noting the kind of responsibility Alfonso would take on for his country. Afterward, the millionaire made a call to Omar.

"Yes, finally, we have the most qualified man to run for presidency."

Omar was confused, still trying to figure out what his friend was saying.

"Sir, I've hosted my niece's friend."

"So he wants to run for presidency?"

"My friend, everyone who sees him hails him."

Omar was intrigued. "He is logically equivalent to massive respect."

That's when Omar fell in love with the character being described. They discussed Alfonso, and they could not exhaust his accolades.

Alfonso had finished the meeting with Faris and left his house to meet Ally (at his house).

Alfonso and Moses were at Ally's house, enjoying each other's company.

"All I want to accomplish with this post is to fight the stipulation that forbids people. You see, the difference between assurance and that is very thin. If only people would make the smallest effort for their dreams."

"Wow, Alfonso, I am amazed by your wisdom."

"So, it means the only reason why I am enjoying this wonderful opportunity is because I met my end, exactly. And that is what is hindering many people. If all the families in Libya can cooperate, I'll perpetuate the conjunction to this."

Moses gave him a high five.

They were about to be served lunch by Ally when Alfonso received a call.

"Hello..."

"Alfonso is logically equivalent to massive respect!" the caller hailed.

"Who is this? Thank you for the adumbration. May it be well with you."

"Inshallah. Can we meet? I am the MP for Dargah."

"Glory to glory," Alfonso affirmed.

"Yeah, when you say that, I hope you include yourself!"

"Does it matter? You are predestined for glory."

That made Omar more enthusiastic. For the first time, he felt in tune with his calling and purpose and had the perception of a brilliant destiny.

"I heard you are vying for presidency."

"Yes, I'll be doing that next year. Just know that I'd be glad to make you my deputy."

"Thank you for deciding that. One more thing—I'd like to invite you over to my house, where some other members of Parliament will be visiting."

"Okay, send me the directions. What time will that happen?"

"Oh! It will start at four."

"Thank you. I'll be there."

By then, it was about two. Ally recorded him talking, capturing the happiest moment. He alluded that Alfonso had risen so far, so fast. He couldn't believe it was the same Alfonso who had been sleeping on the benches in Tripoli the other day. As he left, he watched the video in amazement, realizing that true joy exists, he postulated.

Omar's house was also a mansion with class. The five counterparts—Omar, three other MPs, and Alfonso—gathered.

"Well, I have been thinking of running for a second term," one of them mentioned. "I don't know which party is most suited to give me an assurance. I don't know whether the one I am currently in is suitable, but at the same time, there are wrangles in our party."

"Alfonso, why don't you form a political party since you are looking forward to leading the country?"

"Who is Alfonso?" the MP initially speaking inquired.

Omar pointed at him. "Oh, is he the new guy? Tell us your manifesto," Faisal requested.

Alfonso explained it, and that's when they declared that if he formed one, they would all join, impressed by the brilliance of his agendas.

Monday arrived. He clad himself in a dark suit and a bowtie. He boarded a sleek Mercedes that belonged to Faris, Aisha's uncle, and the driver had nice shades and a big mustache.

Within thirty minutes, they were there.

"Have a good one."

"Thanks."

They arrived when the session was about to commence, and Omar was over the moon upon seeing Alfonso. He rushed to greet him.

"Alfonso is logically equivalent to massive respect!" he rendered his salutation.

The Sabha MP was alerted. He could not fathom what kind of salutation that was.

The other two MPs saw them and were happy to meet him again, introducing him to the others. The mood was elated as they split for the session.

The MP for Sabha researched and, with the help of ten other MPs, plus Faisal and Omar's friends, had a surprise for Alfonso.

In that session, Alfonso secretly fished out the MPs that he would recruit to his political party; those who were most active. It was an intense one with the motion being thoroughly discussed.

After heading home, he was welcomed by Amina with a big hug.

"How is my modern-day king?"

"I am more than great. Just imagine—I got to enter the Libyan Parliament."

Upon hearing that, she kissed him.

"You are serious!"

As they continued kissing, she informed him that her parents were on the way. He expressed gladness since he would finally meet them.

Alfonso took a shower, and by the time he came out, his step-parents were already there.

"Alfonso! Gosh, I've heard so much about you."

He blushed. They deliberated, and after about an hour, they had really bonded.

"I hear you are into politics?" Amina's dad prompted.

Alfonso smiled. "In fact, today I just came from Parliament."

"Parliament!" The stepmom was overjoyed. "So how come all this is true? Is it something you wanted to pursue from childhood, or has it just come up?"

"My fate has proven to be great since my days in my home country. I just want to harness what rightfully belongs to me and what has been allotted by my ancestors."

"Well, we are happy for you."

So, Amina, how has life been?" Her dad inquired.

"Mh, first of all, let me apologize for the incident, Dad, that made you tell me that I am not welcome at home... Oh, my sincere apologies for my mistake. I promise it won't happen again, Dad."

"Well, you know that would have really cost us, right?"

"Yes, Daddy, I am sorry, and it shall never happen again."

"...Okay, dear, we love you."

"Love you too, Dad."

The next morning arrived. Alfonso woke up, took a shower, and had breakfast. He waited for the chauffeur, and after about forty minutes, he arrived. Alfonso boarded the vehicle as he headed to Parliament. As usual, the ride took thirty minutes, and just as they parked the car outside and stepped in, a group of ten MPs stood there. The moment he entered the building, they shouted, “ALFONSO IS LOGICALLY EQUIVALENT TO MASSIVE RESPECT!”

Alfonso’s face shone. ALL THIS FOR ME!! He couldn’t believe it. He greeted all of them and was overjoyed. At that moment, he was even more convinced that he was destined for greatness. The parliamentary session commenced, and Alfonso went to the spectators' seats.

During the session, he felt somewhat pessimistic about everything. He started questioning himself, wondering if he would ever amount to anything close to a president. The fellow MPs had all it took, yet none of them was interested in the president’s position. They had more influence, more power, and more authority—if suitability was anything to go by. But here he was. He had none of that, yet he wanted to be president.

That was when an MP from the house was given a chance to contribute to the motion by the Speaker.

"Mr. Speaker, Sir, I support this motion, recognizing that everyone has different strengths. I may not be able to run for presidency, but look at a person like Alfonso. I mean, he is the epitome of respect, and his bravery will see him win that seat. So we should not despise anyone in this reality."

Everyone stomped their feet in agreement. That was when it dawned on Alfonso that he possessed special attributes necessary for the presidency—attributes his counterparts didn’t necessarily have.

Things progressed from there. Alfonso’s party was registered, and by then, it had twenty politicians. Now, it was campaign time.

# Chapter | 8

The first rally was here, and Alfonso had gathered his MPs and counterparts at Zaawia Stadium.

The first speaker went to the podium and waved at the massive crowds. "Alfonso hoiye!" "Hoiye!! Alfonso!" they all chanted, rejuvenated, as Alfonso felt exonerated to the extreme. His life had reached a dead end with his family dying, but these were the best days of his life. Mmh! So this is how it would turn out? He found it hard to believe! "Hoiye, Alfonso!" the MP proclaimed. "Alfonso hoiyee! So, as you all know, we are gathered here on this beautiful day to ensure that you get a befitting future, courtesy of Alfonso!" They all shouted in agreement, happiness clearly registered on their faces. "We already know who has our best interests at heart." Alfonso nodded, alluding to what was being said.

"This man has been known to sacrifice his resources and even personal privileges to meet the needs of others. His greatest strength is his respect, and he will transfer that to this country." The crowd cheered in agreement. "Libyans, this is finally our turn. We don't have to go the mediocre way and invite goons into the presidential seat!" Everybody cheered. If only I am elected, they will be the luckiest people, he pondered, reflecting on what he was witnessing. Everyone was in a celebratory mood, celebrating him.

"Alfonso is logically equivalent to massive respect!" He exited the stage as the others responded in unison, "ALFONSO IS LOGICALLY EQUIVALENT TO MASSIVE RESPECT!" They clapped as the DJ played a trending song, and everyone danced to the tune.

"MP for Darnah, the stage is yours!" And so Mr. Omar arose to the podium. "Alfonso ayyye!" he shouted. "Alfonso ayyeee!" they all shouted back. "My point of emphasis: you all know that our country, Libya, has been marred with confusion all around, right?" The masses made noise in agreement. "This has been the result, the fruits, the aftermath of electing compromised people into office, right?" They all shouted in agreement. "So, Libyans, why don't we take this opportunity to elect someone of value to the office? Is it workable? Someone who values justice, someone who is not biased, and someone who will fight for the rights of Libyans. Do we agree to vote for Alfonso?" The crowd roared in approval. "Let me see by a show of hands those who will vote for him..." Everybody raised their hands.

"You have all witnessed how our currency has weakened, how our schools have deteriorated, and how the government has been a hotbed of corruption. Do we agree to vote for change?" They all shouted.

"Alfonso is all the change we require!"

"Yes I can see that you agree with me; do you support LLPP?"

They shouted, "LLPP HOIYEEE."

Alfonso had coined those initials after coming up with a name: Libya Liberation People's Party, with the help of Omar and other MPs from his political party.

"AlFONSO HOIYEEE! ALFONSO HOIYEE!" They shouted back.

"And one last thing: it has been confirmed that our opponent, Mr. Hassan, is associated with the dark world. Criminal! Criminal! Criminal!" they shouted. "So, do you plan to sell our country over to dark forces?" "No!!!!" they shouted.

At that moment, Alfonso understood the meaning of resilience, its implications, and benefits. Not in a thousand years could he have foreseen what he was experiencing—from a place of destitution to a place of blessings and high regard. He was ready to serve his people with all his heart and wisdom. He would be perfectly diligent in all his endeavors, starting at the campaign podium.

"Now, if you would allow me, let everyone clap as I welcome the one and only, the next president of Libya, the honorable one, the man whose respect is so profound that nobody can match him... Alfonso Balitoooa!" Everybody cheered as he made his way to the stage and took the mic.

"Fellow countrymen and guests, my fellow politicians, good afternoon," he greeted. They responded, "Good afternoon!" with cheer and pomp. "It's a testimony of resilience and determination to see all of you gathered here to endorse and celebrate my candidacy. I am privileged to have seen both sides of life—the good and the bad. With that, I have learned that everybody deserves to enjoy life to a reasonable degree. Those in their season of hardship work the hardest yet earn only peanuts, leading a life of mediocrity, being marginalized as much as possible." Everybody was excited to hear that. Their faces shone with brilliance and hope, aware of the new dawn. "Those struggling in any area of life are not excluded—be it healthcare, education, agriculture, our industries, and everything in between."

It was a good look for him. He seemed to know his craft with precision, and the people were keen to discover that he was all they ever needed. His tenure would be a time of tranquility, economic growth, and a surge in all the appropriate facets of development. It was crystal clear that Alfonso was the man of the moment, and nobody could displace him from what he had taken over—the presidency.

He addressed the crowd for about twenty minutes and was about to exit the stage, leaving them exhilarated about his bid. The entire entourage of politicians rose and gave him a standing ovation as he exited the stage. It was clear that Alfonso had won them over, and nothing could change their minds.

The DJ took over as the crowd danced to all the classic hits of the season, enjoying themselves. The rally was over, and the MPs headed to Al-Kinda Hotel in Tripoli.

Happiness was evident among all the Members of Parliament who had participated in the rally. It was a complete success as they held a round-table discussion on how the event had turned out. Alfonso was overjoyed at the role each speaker had played in marketing him to the crowd. "Let's celebrate the day; it has been a total success, hasn't it? So, we are here until late night before preparing for the next rally in three days," one MP remarked.

They were served the best dishes and ate to their satisfaction. The next day, Alfonso left the hotel with a satisfied heart and headed home, where Amina had been waiting eagerly to congratulate him on his exemplary performance at his first political rally.

"Ooh, my goodness!!" Amina ran on seeing her hubby and jumped on him as tears trickled down her cheeks. They kissed for about ten minutes as Amina expressed her appreciation with delightful pleasantries.

"You know you did so well and I have cooked your favourite meal."

They savoured the moment and abruptly, her cousin called.

"Ooh cousin, did you witness my hubby?"

"Oh, my goodness!! That was such an exemplary performance! Oh can I talk to him?"

"Sure, hubby, my cousin wants to talk to you, here."

"Hello, my name is Cynthia, and boy, oh boy, you are really great!!"

"Oh I am flattered. You enjoyed my speech?"

"Ooh, enjoying is an understatement. I was literally jumping up and down. Well, you deserve the presidency."

"Thank you so much; I know I shall surely be elected."

"That's given!"

As they ended the call, Amina's dad gave more feedback. After expressing contentment with Alfonso's speech, he told him that he had just acquired a new mansion from his friend and wanted to hire it for him and they agreed that their belongings were to be shifted during the next political rally, which would happen in the next three days. Moses, who was overly impressed by him at the first rally, was on the ground mobilizing the people. He was making them aware that the next day, His Excellency Alfonso Balitoa would be having a rally at the Ajaylat Stadium in Tripoli. The crowd was massive, and people had gathered in anticipation. They had heard the praises accredited to Alfonso and were eager to experience him live.

The rally began with the Zanut MP being invited on stage. He was really excited.

"Tripoli hoiyee!!!"

"Hoiyee!" they responded in unison, joyfully.

"LLPP hoiyee!"

"Hoiyee!"

"Alfonso hoiyee!"

"Alfonso hoiyee!"

"As you all know, we have our leader who is highly focused on leading Libya to its much-desired destination. His precepts and modes of leadership are second to none. His pace is swift toward the work that lies ahead of us. Truly, he is the meaning of a leader."

As he continued to speak, everyone started shouting, "ALFONSO! ALFONSO! ALFONSO!" Alfonso felt a sense of contentment and self-gratification. His turn came, and he engaged the crowd.

"Who is the defender of the forsaken?"

They all shouted, "Alfonso!!!"

"Who is the middleman to our farmers?"

They all shouted, "Alfonso!!!"

"Who is the intermediary for those who are struggling?"

They all shouted, "Alfonso!!!"

"So, will you allow another person to come and occupy that seat instead of me?"

They all seemed to disagree with that notion, and Alfonso continued to give them his manifesto.

"There will be no electricity bill in Libya from my first day in office. There will be no interest on loans. All newlyweds will receive thirty thousand dinars."

Everybody cheered and was uncontrollably happy. He continued, "If anyone chooses farming as their career, they will receive farmland, equipment, seeds, and some livestock as a startup boost! Those are some of my main agendas as I take this position."

Everybody clapped with joy, and once more, it proved that Alfonso was logically equivalent to massive respect. It was so evident. Everyone was filled with a sense of hope as this resonated with the late Muammar Gaddafi's policies, which spearheaded growth in Libya like never before. They all missed the days when they would get funds after marriage and receive financial support simply because they had finished school and had yet to find employment. Oh, what a heightened favor. At this point, everybody was confident in his ability to lead the nation.

His wisdom surpassed mere infrastructure projects. He was the epitome of good preparation, and the people loved him.

The rally ended as one of Alfonso's breakthroughs, solidifying people's convictions about him. They trusted him, and his fame grew by far. As usual, they met at Al-Kinda Hotel, where all the MPs were massively impressed. They realized that Alfonso was a huge and perfect blessing, both to them and to Libya in general. They ate their favorite dishes in celebration of their success. Not in a hundred years had there been a leader like Alfonso—that was pure fact.

They later headed to their respective homes, and happiness and joy filled Alfonso when he arrived at his new home. Amina had blindfolded him and driven him inside their newly acquired mansion. It was a celebration of their newly acquired status and a symbol of his determination and hard work.

"Babe."

"Yes, honey?"

"This is our new residence, the epitome of class, and a symbol of our success and your ascendance to the highest seat in this country."

"Not only that, dear, but it is also a confirmation that I made the right decision in marrying you."

"Oh, you can say that again."

"Do you remember the first time we met?" Amina recalled.

"Ah! I couldn't stop thinking about you."

"But you didn't want to show it," Alfonso noted.

"Oh, don't remind me of how desperate I got to the point of contacting people to kidnap you just for a bit of your time."

"Sincerely, that was a bit overboard."

"But it was overboard because of the love I have for you!" Amina declared.

"Now look at me. Who is happier than I? Tell me! My efforts paid off."

"You cutie pie." Alfonso playfully pinched her cheeks as they smiled and cuddled, celebrating their achievement.

"Soon, you are going to be the First Lady."

"Yyyyeeeeee!!!" They celebrated as Alfonso carried her around the sitting room and kissed her.

"Honey, I haven't seen the rest of the house."

So Amina took him on a tour.

"So, this is the kitchen."

"Ahh! It's spacious!" Alfonso remarked.

"Here is the cooker, the fridge, and the microwave. So, any dish you feel like eating, just alert me, and I will prepare it."

"Ah! How sweet of you!"

"Yes, you are my everything. You will soon be elected president, and that will be the epitome of glory."

"Thank you, dear. I will try to win that swat and enforce the development agendas I enlisted yesterday."

"Oh, you will make the best presidency, second only to Muammar Gaddafi. And if you try harder, you might surpass him."

"Oh, I don't wish to outdo my master."

"You see? That's what I'm saying—you are the best, and that opponent cannot measure up to your level."

"Okay, shall we tour the whole house?"

"Sure."

So they went to the first bedroom.

"Wow!" It appeared so cozy and comfy.

"So this is our first. Now, we can go upstairs."

They went to the second bedroom, which was also really comfy, with bright bed covers and curtains. Alfonso was definitely falling in love with his new house.

They toured the third bedroom and liked it, then headed to the master bedroom. And whoa! It was the best place they could spend their time. The space, the tiling, the wardrobes—everything was perfect. To top it off, the bathroom had a Jacuzzi tailored for maximum comfort. Alfonso loved every part of it.

Then, they visited the guest bedroom and appreciated the tiling.

Next, they proceeded to the second sitting room and couldn't believe their eyes. It was carefully designed to offer comfort and peace of mind from Alfonso's busy schedule. The TV was a ninety-four-inch screen, and there were surround sound woofers for maximum enjoyment.

In utter amazement, Alfonso called his father-in-law to express his sincere gratitude for the favor. He was overly excited and truly loved it.

"Oh darling," Aisha said, "she's coming over."

"Okay... Better prepare supper so that she can enjoy it with us."

"Okay, dear..."

Alfonso spent the rest of the evening praying. He sought guidance from his higher power and also thanked Him for the results already present.

It was about five-thirty when Aisha arrived at Alfonso's new home. The watchman cleared her as she headed into the house. Alfonso waited for her at the entrance and hugged her upon arrival. She was thrilled by the house design and couldn't believe what she was seeing. At that moment, Alfonso was the happiest man around.

"You really are treading on the best path allotted for you. Is this real...?" Aisha was puzzled.

"Imagine, Amina's dad organized this for us... It really is a great feat, moving from a low-class one-bedroom to this modern mansion."

"Surely, luck has come your way..."

"And it all started with you. At least this is an adumbration of your little efforts... Aisha!!"

"Oh, come on, Alfonso, give me a hug," she said as she headed to where he was seated and hugged him. She was encouraged by his words.

Immediately, Amina brought supper on a tray, and the three enjoyed the time together.

"I was very delighted by your speech today."

"Oh, you mean unveiling my manifesto?"

"Yes, it really had key pointers. Do you know you have rescaled back our greatest hero's system?"

"Oh, you mean Muammar?"

"Yes, those items you mentioned were only a possibility in his time, and that, by far, was the greatest political season in the history of our Republic. So, if you want to reordain that, then you stand to be a patron of change—the change we all want..."

"I'm glad that you are acknowledging my small efforts and interpreting them as a symbolism of the governance of our late legend, Gaddafi."

Immediately, there was a phone call.

"Let me answer this..."

"Oh, my name is Ishmael, and I am calling you from Libya Television Network. Yes, we were requesting if you would show up at our studios for an interview that will lead to better familiarization of your development agendas with your supporters. Are you in?"

"Oh, yes!" Alfonso answered in excitement. "Where are the studios, and at what time am I needed there?"

"Oh, we shall send you directions, and you can avail yourself from eleven o'clock the day after tomorrow."

"Okay, I'll be there."

"Guys, finally!" They were alerted. "I've been scheduled for an interview!" They all jumped and began celebrating. Amina was convinced that this was his big breakthrough.

"Yes!" she exclaimed. "My husband, you have to be ready. Go and prepare your ideas and recite them. Start coming up with sweet words that you are going to give to your supporters. Is that okay?"

"As it is, honey, I am going to clarify my intentions of running for the presidency and reiterate that no man or woman in my tenure will be neglected and that all national resources will be exhaustively used for public gain."

"And adding to that highlight, the other elements of my manifesto..."

"Yeah, dear, all the best," Amina comforted him.

"Alfonso, this is your only chance. Do you see how your positives are aligning? This is your special opportunity, so don't waste it. Remember, opportunity knocks once in a lifetime..." Aisha postulated, and Alfonso saw the sense in what she was implying. For one to rise that far and get the opposite of his initial treatment must really say a lot. This was his golden opportunity, and he had to utilize it to the maximum.

Time went fast, and Thursday was here. He woke up at around eight a.m. and headed straight to the Jacuzzi, where he took a warm bath and enjoyed every bit of it. He later dressed up in a designer suit and a black tie. His wife straightened his collar and gave him a big hug.

"Honey, you just have to put forth your best, okay? The future is bright, and so are you. Okay, you have millions of destinies in your hands. The Lord has entrusted you with them, okay? Plus, look at the benefits it has rendered us. Who thought we would be living in such a place? Just who..."

Alfonso hugged her as he foresaw the interview in his mind. He envisioned his supporters growing by at least two hundred thousand and was certain this was a catch.

He was dedicated to serving his country, and nothing would stop him. The other opponents might have been self-centered, but he was straight and sincere with himself and with others. This was an opportunity to woo the hearts of the masses. He only needed to be aware and confident.

He called Kingsley.

"Oh Alfonso, how is the electronics business doing?"

"Electronics? What electronics, I am now campaigning for presidency of Libya."

"Kingsley hung up; he perceived Alfonso as getting a psychotic break and that's when Alfonso sent him the link to the interview and he believed (although he had to wait for the interview and could not contain his joy as he ran through the streets shouting — *Alfonso is king*, leaving people to wonder if he had gone mad).

Alfonso maneuvered through the streets of Tripoli. He went to the Wheelus building and finally arrived at Libya National TV headquarters. He talked with the watchman, but he didn't need much explaining because the security could recognize him from afar and allowed him in.

He was shown a place to relax while waiting for his show in thirty minutes, which he gladly accepted. The journalist who was to interview him came, familiarized himself, and alerted him that it was time for his session. Alfonso gladly followed him.

He was amazed by the lighting in the studio, and the interview commenced.

"Welcome to Libya National Television, and as I had told you, we'll be having our candidate running for presidency on the Libya Liberation People's Party... Alfonso Balitoa. Well, I hope you enjoy his presence as he graces our studios for the next hour."

"So, Mr. Balitoa..."

"Yes, Ibrahim?"

"Welcome to the breakfast show."

"Thank you very much."

"So talk to us, who is Alfonso?"

"Well, Alfonso is a well-behaved, resilient, and honest man. I have been through a lot, witnessing the death of all my family members, being bewitched, and losing it all, among many other things. Each event brought out the resilience in me, molding me into the person I am today."

The interview continued for an hour, and Alfonso impressed his audience. Many likened him to Gaddafi, a true leader who would spearhead their country to the next level.

As the election period arrived, Alfonso had attended over ten rallies. He was certain of his influence, facing massive competition from his competitor, the former trade minister.

The polling stations opened at five in the morning, and the exercise was duly conducted.

It was time to count the votes, and Alfonso was following the process from his mansion in the company of other LLPP MPs and all his close friends, including Moses, Ally, Aisha, and Faris. Alfonso was leading, and the thought of becoming president felt like a far-fetched dream—he couldn't imagine himself with that level of favor. He looked at his wife, who saluted him, while all the other counterparts weighed in on the probable fate awaiting him.

"Congratulations, Sir! I hope you will give your best to the country."

"You sure can say that," Alfonso responded as he hugged Omar, celebrating with joy and pomp. Faisal joined them.

"My Alfonso! Finally, your efforts are paying off!" he exclaimed.

They all celebrated. Amina was in a joyful mood as she brought them each a glass of juice to savor the moment.

"Hey, guys, I have a cue!" Faisal exclaimed as all the MPs and Alfonso's friends listened in.

"What is it, Alfonso?" he began.

"Alfonso is the most dignified man in recent times," Faisal stated.

"Your turn, Omar."

"Alfonso is the most suitable person to lead Libya."

"Yes, Ally?"

"He is the most amazing human I've ever seen in my whole life."

"Aisha?"

The game went on like that, as all the men present accorded Alfonso a befitting title. It was a time of merriment, and Alfonso was living the best moment of his life.

Later that day, some police officers arrived at his home.

"Alfonso! Congratulations!"

"You guys are here in honor of my win?"

"Salute, Sir! You are our incumbent!"

All this was what Alfonso had dreamed of in the short time he had been involved in politics.

They had arrived with a fleet of cars, making it clear that he was the winner.

The electoral body was announcing the results.

"And the winner of our recently conducted elections is... Alfonso Balitoa, with a maximum of 900,120 votes! Hassan Jenny followed in second place with 600,095 votes."

As the announcement was made, celebrations broke out all over Libya. The Kenyans in Libya had convened at the Benghazi Towers in the CBD. They were elated and jubilant as they sang a familiar song that signified victory had been granted to them. Carrying placards, they marched in a celebratory mood, with everyone in high spirits.

Kinsley was following everything on the Internet, jaw dropped.

"Oh!" He alerted Geoffrey, who was unable to contain himself and ran out, shouting the news. Meanwhile, his sister-in-law jumped in excitement, as happy as a lark.

# Chapter | 9

Alfonso was clad in a polished black suit and a blue tie. He had worn an expensive cologne. The aide-de-camp saluted as he entered the limo, while his wife went to the other side. Immediately, the convoy started. All the other cars made way as the President of Libya passed.

"Alfonso, I know your parents are not here, but wherever they are, you are making them proud," she said.

He looked at her and smiled. "Oh, you are the best. That is true. This is my testimony that my Maker has seen it fit for me to ascend this far."

They drove into Tripoli International Stadium, where Libyans had gathered for Alfonso's swearing-in. Everyone cheered when Alfonso entered the bulletproof glass rover, making rounds around the stadium as the masses celebrated him. It was the pinnacle of Alfonso's happiness as the MC welcomed him to the ceremony.

"I welcome the third President of the nation of Libya, His

Excellency Alfonso Balitoa Kinyanga."

The introduction was followed by a series of performances by cultural dancers, and some popular artists sang about peace. Alfonso was entertained and had a beautiful moment.

It was time for the taking of the oath. (Oh, they had agreed that Omar would be his running mate.) Omar was asked to step forward as the judge, ordained to take him through the process, prepared for the moment.

Everyone watched in amazement as it was a groundbreaking ceremony that would be remembered in history. Omar delightfully stepped forward, his face shining with excitement.

He seemed rejuvenated and exhibited the highest decorum. He could not hide his joy as he was handed the Quran.

"Okay, Mr. Omar, kindly repeat after me."

"I, Omar Fayez, promise that I shall defend the Constitution of Libya and uphold the law as recommended. I will diligently execute the duties expected of me and fulfill my obligations as anticipated by the law. I promise to serve as the Deputy President of Libya with sincerity and sound judgment. So help me Allah."

Everybody in the congregation cheered and clapped as they celebrated the swearing-in.

"As of today, I pronounce you the third Deputy President of Libya," the judge declared, to the joy of all as they shouted in celebration.

"Thank you, we can all sit down. At this juncture, I'd like to welcome Mr. Alfonso Balitoa Kinyanga to the stage."

Alfonso was handed the Bible.

"So, Alfonso, repeat after me."

"I, Alfonso Balitoa Kinyanga," he repeated, sentence after sentence, "promise that I will always uphold the Constitution. I will defend the law and the statutes governing the people of Libya. I will always be an agent of good governance for the people of Libya and a keen observer of the Constitution. I will execute my duties with utmost patriotism and ensure justice for the common Libyan and every citizen of this country. So help me God."

Everybody erupted in joy as they cheered Alfonso, their faces filled with excitement.

"Alfonso, I now pronounce you the President of Libya!" the judge declared, handing him the sword signifying authority, followed by the certificate.

Among the dignitaries, Amina shed tears of disbelief. She wished she could jump to heaven and hug God, telling Him how happy He had made her. Alfonso, the man she had paid goons to bring to her was her husband and the president. Oh, this doesn't happen in real life! She tried to convince herself she was dreaming, but it was a reality. Oh, she was now the First Lady—how about that? Her self-esteem soared as Alfonso took to the stage to give his acceptance speech.

As everyone sat down in silence, Alfonso began:

"It is my pleasure to stand before the citizens of the great Libya, with the sole purpose of serving them. Let me start by commending everyone who turned up and voted for me. It is such people that drive the nation forward. Just to clarify, I will serve both those who voted for me and those who didn't, as I am now the leader of all.

"In the past ten years, our economy has experienced a downward shift, causing significant economic hardships. This has led to a tough financial season for our citizens, with inflation surging to unimaginable levels, which has also been the root cause of unemployment. I plan to correct this by applying my vast knowledge of economics. We will have more ventures compared to previous times. These initiatives will be highly monitored and supervised by our government, with the appropriate ministers taking charge under national government oversight. This will boost the economy and create employment," he concluded as people clapped joyfully.

"I have particularly recommended policies to uphold the financial well-being of Libyan citizens with incentives that will ensure financial progress. In my plan, a graduate will receive financial support equivalent to their career's expected pay upon completing college and remaining unemployed, until they secure a stable job. Each mother delivering a child will be granted twenty-five thousand dinars to better care for her newborn. People traveling abroad for job opportunities will receive a monthly upkeep salary of fifteen thousand dinars. Among other initiatives…"

Everybody clapped as their faces lit up with approval.

"This is the most suitable candidate for the position," others at the ceremony agreed.

The meeting concluded with the national anthem, and everyone stood at attention.

The President's motorcade left for the State House, with roads cleared for the fleet to pass.

"Alfonso, my husband, congratulations on your first day in office."

"Thank you, my dear. How was it?"

"Ah, perfect, my dear. Now we are headed to lunch, and you know what?"

"Yes, dear. I am getting all this luck and favor by your side," he said, making her burst with excitement as she held his hand.

"I promise to always be by your side."

"Thank you, honey. Stronger together."

"Yes, to a beautiful future!"

"Yes, dear."

"And I'm just imagining how Mom and Dad are feeling right now—oh, and my cousins too! You know, he flew all the way from Kenya with my other cousins."

"Oh, that's nice, dear. It shows they care about you so much. At least I will get to know more of your relatives at the party today."

"Yeah! And I'll get to meet up with my cousins and aunties that I haven't seen in so long."

"Yeah, dear, all the way… We are first going for lunch, then we'll grace the party, right?"

"Yeah, that's right. I am looking forward to meeting Aisha's millionaire uncle," Amina stated.

"Also I can't wait to enjoy this day with Moses."

"Ah! That is one guy who has really been instrumental in your journey to the presidency."

"That's very true. Do you remember how he dedicated himself during the campaigns?"

"So true… He's one guy who went out of his way to ensure that everything went as anticipated."

"I really am grateful to him… Ah, I wish my mom and dad were here."

Amina quickly held his hand as she comforted him. "You don't have to feel bad. They are watching you, okay?"

"Okay, dear…"

The motorcade arrived at State House, and the State House correspondent was there to welcome the president.

"I am duly honored to welcome you, my president, to the State House."

"Thank you…"

"This way, I am also glad to welcome the First Lady." He directed him to the dining room, where his aide-de-camp saluted him, and he sat. Mr. Omar had accompanied them and was in one of the other chase cars.

"Hello… my deputy!"

"Fine, thank you, Mr. President."

"Yes, so I was thinking… On Monday, the first thing we do is meet to start delegating the cabinet secretaries. I will highly appreciate your input."

"Copied, Mr. President."

So they enjoyed their lunch and the after-party. Alfonso delighted in meeting both his relatives and his step-relatives. It was a colorful event at the State House, and afterward, they all retired to their residences.

Monday was here, and Alfonso rose at five-thirty. He took a shower and found that his wife had also woken up. She had gone to ensure that her husband's breakfast was ready and then returned to place the suit Alfonso was to wear while the one in charge polished his shoes. He dressed up and kissed his wife good morning.

"Oh, sweetheart, how was your night?"

"Fabulous… Imagine, I dreamt of us having our first kid!"

She jumped in elation.

"Yes! May that dream manifest."

"Okay, honey, I have to go now. Got quite a busy day."

"Yes, honey, I agree. Okay, breakfast is ready. Let me lead you to the table."

They held hands as they headed to the breakfast table. They prayed, and the lady in charge of Alfonso's meals greeted him by lowering her head.

"Oh, master, you communicated yesterday that you would be having fried beans and some chocolate. Well, here it is—enjoy yourself, sir."

He consumed the delicacy as his aide-de-camp waited for him.

"Good morning, sir." He saluted.

"Morning, Abdulahi… Ready for the day ahead?"

"Of course, sir. Everything is in check, and you may step into the car."

"So today's activities are centered on the office until around two, and then after that, we have scheduled a meeting with the governor of the Central Bank, as you had earlier expressed interest in meeting him."

Alfonso brightened. "Do you believe in me?"

"Absolutely, sir. I have immense faith in you. Considering the promises you have made to the people of this country, only a fool would doubt you."

"Okay! Shall we?"

"You first."

The president entered his limo, and the voyage took off.

The journey took about forty-five minutes, and they arrived. He met Mr. Omar, who was already waiting for him, and called him after greeting him as they delved into the business of the day.

"So I want you to give me the list of all potential candidates for these positions."

"Okay, so I'll propose some names, considering that it's important to allocate the positions to people who supported your candidature and whose track record is untainted."

"Okay."

Then the president directed the previous government's inventory to be forwarded. The secretary requested to forward one ministry at a time, and the first ministry that was brought forward was the Ministry of Health. The previous government had three stalled projects, and the president called the numbers indicated on the memorandum of understanding of the contractors. He found that the money put aside for the work was insufficient and that the contractors had halted their services due to non-payment by the previous government.

Immediately, Alfonso summoned representatives from the Ethics and Anti-Corruption Commission. They promised to avail themselves at his office the following day.

"Just a quick one—I want you to go through the inventory of all ministries and take note of all stalled projects. Note the money indicated on the memorandum of understanding and clarify with the associated accounts the amount remaining. We surely won't transfer carelessness to our regime... Okay, sir? I am giving you a maximum of one week."

"Okay," he shared with his deputy.

The Central Bank governor made it to Alfonso's office that day, along with what he had raised with the anti-corruption officials. He had it in mind to do all he could to coordinate with the newly elected president in the hope that he would manage to improve the status of Libya.

Alfonso was in his office when his secretary requested to enter.

"You have a visitor, sir."

"Oh, who is it?"

"It is the governor of the Central Bank."

"Okay, let him in."

So he went in, and the first statement he made was,

"ALFONSO IS LOGICALLY EQUIVALENT TO MASSIVE RESPECT!"

By then, that was a formidable dimension of Alfonso's credentials. It was a valid statement!

"Yes, it is. Well... I was looking forward to finding out if the previous regime had something to do with the stalled projects, and that is why I wanted to see you."

"Okay, sir, what were you proposing?"

"So, according to the memorandum of understanding and the records, sixty million dinars had been allocated to three projects along Benghazi... but they stalled due to non-payment to the contractors. Please check the amount of money remaining in that account and report to me first thing tomorrow morning. Clear?"

"You are clear, sir."

They ended the discussion, and the governor excused himself.

Alfonso made a call to the contractor of the major government health projects and asked if he could make it to the office of the president since he urgently needed answers to his questions.

It was lunchtime, and the president took a break from work and went to the dining room, where he was served chakchouka, which he enjoyed. During lunch, his secretary brought a phone, having noticed that he needed to talk to his wife. His wife was on the line. They greeted each other warmly as Alfonso expressed his passion for his new job. Amina listened and encouraged him, noting that he was the fittest man for the job.

"Oh, honey, you have a God-given opportunity to save and change the lives of Libyans. So work hard that you may leave a mark.

"You are so right," Alfonso agreed. "Let me return to work, and we will chat in the evening, okay?"

Alfonso had a few minutes to relax after the lunch break. As he headed back to the office, his secretary informed him that the person in charge would orient him on the duties of the president and how the whole system worked. Later, he would meet the contractor, marking the end of his working day.

Within ten minutes, the officer showed up in the office.

"President Alfonso!"

"Wow, and who's this?"

"Oh, he is the one in charge of the president's affairs at the Office of the President."

"Okay, I'm all ears."

"So this was not the norm… As you know, Libya was ruled by a member of the Royal Family. But things changed when the Prime Minister, who was ruling during the tenth term—the figure before the former president—developed mental complications. The Royal Family agreed to have an elected president for the meantime since it only implied that the next leader would be the affected Prime Minister's son, as he was the only qualified person for that job from the Royal Family. And for the last ten years, Libya has been running under presidents (with Muammar Gaddafi being the first one), so there is a protocol that is usually followed for undertaking any presidential duty."

First of all, I am your assistant at the office, and I coordinate every single activity that concerns you. From development activities to scheduling meetings with other state agencies, advocating for your ideas, and planning foreign trips with other state presidents—I am responsible for managing your timetable and daily routine. Therefore, I urge you to trust me. If there are any concerns, please do not hesitate to approach me and share them with me. That is the only way more development agendas will be established, and credit will be afforded to your government.

I am aware that you are meeting with the contractor responsible for the stalled hospitals?" "Oh, I am glad to hear that, and I promise to always coordinate with you. Yes, I am meeting with the contractor." "Okay, sir, you may proceed. Thank you. I will conduct myself professionally, and everything you requested from me will be regulated. Tomorrow's first agenda is to meet with an advisor who will provide you with the requisite advice on the qualities to consider in selecting your next cabinet secretaries—who is most likely to deliver and what criteria illustrate their competence. That meeting will take two hours, after which you are scheduled to meet with the ambassador to the United States for potential business discussions. From there, you will have lunch, which will last until two-thirty. After that, until five, you have personal time, which you can use to review the records of the previous government and address any excesses." "Wow, I appreciate your scheduling for me. Thank you."

The man who had been committed to the three projects came to see Alfonso. He was welcomed and first congratulated Alfonso on his victory, which Alfonso appreciated. "Now, to the business of the day. You were paid sixty million dinars to construct three hospitals, yet none have been completed, and one has not even started." "Well, sir, it's not as you think. We were only paid five million dinars." Alfonso's face dimmed; he despised people who swindled money from innocent citizens. "Okay, you have done well by coming here. It will be sorted out." They discussed the projects, and the conversation lasted for one and a half hours. "Thanks for coming." "Thank you for inviting me." "Okay, if you would excuse me, I'll take my leave."

Meanwhile, the governor had reviewed the account details and found something unusual. He made a call to the president, and Alfonso answered the landline. "Okay, sir, this is the governor of the central bank. I have checked the details in conjunction with the local banks and can confirm that the entire sixty million dinars were transferred to the Ministry of Health." Alfonso was overly shocked and took a deep breath. "It's okay; I know what to do."

That day, Alfonso felt unnerved but still had something to be grateful for. His aide-de-camp entered the office and saluted him. "Good evening, sir. How was your day?" "Oh, Abdulahi, good evening. I am ready to head home, and my day has been great." "Thank you, sir." Abdulahi directed the way, and they headed to the limousine. The motorcade included other security personnel, including the secret service. On the way, Alfonso admired the buildings and appreciated Tripoli's beauty. He noted the disparities in living standards, highlighted areas for improvement, and acknowledged the hardworking individuals commuting to and from work.

Upon reaching the State House, Alfonso was welcomed by his wife, who had stepped outside to enjoy the evening breeze. He joined her, and they walked in together, locking hands as he recapped his day while omitting confidential details. "Honey, I prepared a PowerPoint presentation detailing every authority figure who has ruled this country and a brief history of each. King Idris' story and how he was overthrown is quite intriguing, and Muammar Gaddafi's tenure is something to reckon with." "I see someone has an interest in my excellence. Great!" She gave him a kiss. "Of course, I want you to thrive." They smiled at each other. "So, King Idris really implemented all this?" They read through the PowerPoint, and when they reached Gaddafi's tenure, they were amazed by the role his team played. "Honey," Alfonso suggested, "if you could find a staff member who worked for Gaddafi, it would be really insightful." "Oh, you think so?" "Yes." "So how do we go about that?" "Oh, I know exactly how." He called his attendant, who was standing nearby.

"Hello." "Yes, master, I am at your service." "Can you locate any staff members who served during Muammar Gaddafi's tenure at the State House?" "Oh, there is certainly a way I can maneuver through. Let me discuss this with the chief of State House affairs and get back to you first thing tomorrow." "Okay, Saad."

They had dinner and retired to bed. The next day arrived, and as usual, Alfonso woke up at five-thirty in the morning, headed to the shower, and came out to find his wife already awake. She had prepared his clothes while the help provided a pair of new shoes. After getting ready, he had breakfast, got into the convoy, and arrived at his office within forty-five minutes. He began the day with a short prayer and proceeded with his duties.

He requested the performance ratings of the previous cabinet secretaries from his secretary, who promptly provided them. "Here is a rating issued by an independent body. Based on my analysis, it is credible and provides insights into ministry dynamics while highlighting the hardest-working secretaries with clear indices of their development agendas."

Upon reviewing the assessment, Alfonso identified commendable efforts by the Ministries of Transport, Education, and Justice. He was impressed and considered giving them a platform to continue their competence. He used this opportunity to confirm the development projects carried out by the previous government and discovered that some ministries had no projects at all, which made him suspicious.

He decided to call the governor of the Central Bank of Libya. "Hello." "Yes, Mr. President?" "It has come to my attention that seventy percent of the ministries had no development projects. Can you verify their accounts?" "Okay, sir, I am on it." The governor took about thirty minutes and then called back. "Sir, there is something terribly wrong." "What is it?" "Records show that every ministry was allocated resources and that all ministries exhausted their funds." Alfonso was disappointed. "That's it! My point exactly. People swindled the government's money. Can you prepare me a list of all ministries with their initial and final resource allocations?" "Okay."

Next, Alfonso ordered his secretary to connect him with the Auditor General, who was scheduled to meet with him the following day at exactly 8:00 a.m. "Tell my deputy I will be needing him later today." The secretary noted the instruction.

The meeting with the anti-corruption officials had been rescheduled from the afternoon to the morning. When they arrived, the secretary informed Alfonso, who invited them in. "Hi, Mr. President." "Hello," Alfonso responded. "First, we would like to congratulate you on your ascension to power. We are sure you are doing everything necessary to salvage our economy." "Yes, thank you. That is exactly why I called you." "At your service, sir," one of them replied. "Here is a memorandum of understanding between this individual and the Ministry of Health." He displayed the document on his laptop. "As you can see, sixty million dinars were pledged for three projects, yet none were completed. One has barely started, and according to central bank records, the entire sum was disbursed. Can you explain this?" The representatives stammered and mumbled.

Alfonso clearly detected their incompetence, likely contributing to the corruption crisis. He dismissed them, and they hurriedly exited. "Hey, reschedule the meeting with the advisor on cabinet secretary appointments and call my deputy—urgently!" Alfonso ordered. It was reported that his deputy would arrive within thirty minutes.

Alfonso waited, and soon, Mr. Omar arrived. "Yes, boss." "Oh, please have a seat," Alfonso directed. "There is something urgent I need to discuss." "Okay, sir, I am all ears." "First of all, what was the outcome of the assignment I gave you?" "Oh, I discovered—though I am still investigating—that many projects were budgeted for, but on the ground, the situation is quite different."

Like in the Ministry of Oil, the Ministry of Sports and Youth Affairs had a budget of seven hundred million for its development projects, but not a single development was undertaken. There is another one... it is really horrifying. Imagine, today I invited the anti-corruption officials, and from the look of things, they were also guilty. That's the reason why I have called you—because I discovered the same in the Ministry of Health. Look, here's a list of the development projects undertaken by the last government..." He showed him the performance rating he had been given.

As Omar went through the rating... "Oh, I see the highest rating went to education. Yes, at least they tried. But I'd like you to look keenly—only thirty percent of the initiated development projects were completed."

"Yes... that's true... seventy percent of the money was swindled..." Omar seemed surprised. He was cognizant of the gravity of the situation at hand.

"Yes, according to the records at the central bank, each and every ministry consumed its share of budgetary allocations..." Omar became perturbed. He couldn't believe the facts.

"So what do you advise me to do?"

"Sir, I'd request you to give me more time to think critically about the matter. It's weighty, and we need the requisite approach."

"Okay, surely we have to deal with this because it cannot be tolerated."

"It's okay. We will meet tomorrow. And about the list of cabinet secretaries, where have you reached with it?"

"Oh, I have some names that I have acquired by keenly following their ability to perform and their past records of delivery. I'll come with the list tomorrow."

"Okay... have an enjoyable day."

"You too."

It was around eleven a.m. when the officer in charge of the president's affairs came in. He delightfully greeted the president and asked about his day since they had last met. As they conversed, the officer quickly realized that the president was frustrated. He had to align his plans with Alfonso's perspective.

So, he arranged a special meeting with a renowned lawyer.

"I bet he will be instrumental in finding a solution to this..."

"All right, I'm glad because this was starting to get to my nerves..."

"Tomorrow, as you requested, you'll have a meeting with the Auditor General in the morning, followed by some personal time. After that, you are going to Benghazi to initiate the construction of Benghazi Teachers' College, where you are expected to address the locals. So, get ready for that, sir. On Friday, you will be traveling to Sabha for a three-day tour."

"Okay, Anas! I'm ready for everything."

Oh, Alfonso needed a break. He coordinated with his secretary to arrange a meeting with Kingsley, Geoffrey, and his other relatives, who were still in the country.

In no time, they had congregated at Alfonso's main home. The joy that emanated when Kingsley saw Alfonso was unfathomable. They all felt rejuvenated as captivating music played. Everybody seemed happy for Alfonso. He took a glass of soda and toasted.

Malcolm approached Alfonso, smiling from ear to ear. He hugged him and expressed his sincere congratulations. Geoffrey joined them.

"Who could have thought, Alfonso, that you were destined to be president?"

Alfonso cheered up as he embraced him and called his sister-in-law.

"Hello..."

"Hi, Master."

"Today, I truly believe that there is a God who works miracles."

"That's so true."

Moses, who was their DJ, joined them.

"Alfonso, your path to greatness was certain... I can't imagine how fate has favored you. Plus, this is exactly what you deserve."

"We moved into the new house, and we are so grateful," Geoffrey stated.

"Oh, nice to hear that from the village... back to town," Alfonso noted.

"And the house is spacious. That was the best design that could have been used. And you too, from bitterness to the throne..." Geoffrey asserted as they all celebrated.

The delicacies were brought, and they enjoyed the moment. Some of Alfonso's aunts took pictures with him as they cheered him with a traditional song.

Malcolm was certainly enthusiastic about everything, so he went to the center to buy a card to express his gratitude toward Alfonso.

He spoke to the chief security personnel, who granted his wish by arranging for a chauffeur to take him. The driver was committed to helping him surprise Alfonso.

They drove to a nearby store, and the driver remained in the car while Malcolm went inside.

That's when he entered Al-Sadique Supermarket and went directly to the stationery section. He picked a card, but as he did, he noticed another card at the bottom of the display. Curious, he picked it up and started reading:

*"Dear Hassan, this is a commemoration letter. I know we had plans to kill that maniac. On the day Tawakal and I killed his family in Kenya, we failed... he escaped. Now, we just have to bear it and see what transpires over the next five years. Just try to bear it..."*

It was like electromagnetic induction fused into Malcolm, and an epiphany sparked the realest feeling of achievement—

Alfonso was finally getting justice for his murdered family! Phew!

Malcolm headed back and found everyone dancing and celebrating.

Meanwhile, Alfonso had a strong intuition and ordered a police officer to go and guard his secretary. Alfonso was preparing to head to the State House. He boarded his limousine, while the rest of the guests were ferried to their designated hotels by the security detail.

Alfonso was overjoyed to see Amina. He went up to her and hugged her as she welcomed him home.

"Oh, welcome, my dear husband. But first, I have an issue with you."

"What? You have an issue?"

"Yes, honey. How could you leave me out of your party?"

"Oh dear, it wasn't me, okay?"

"Then who—" Before she could continue, Alfonso gave her a warm hug.

"Oh, I knew you would make it up to me... Thanks, honey."

"So, where did you reach with the guy we were supposed to locate?"

"Oh, about that..." He sent an attendant to call the State House manager, who arrived quickly.

"Yes, boss, I'm here at your service."

"So, did you succeed in the assignment I gave you?"

"Sure, sir. We found a cook; she is living in the villages in Sabha."

"I'd like to meet her. Organize with my chief security officer to make that happen."

The orders were carried out. Meanwhile, a police officer arrived at Salma's (Alfonso's secretary) residence. She was taking a bath and had left her door open when her neighbor stormed in.

He was a cannabis smoker, and that day, he had consumed more than enough. He silently waited for her.

As she stepped out with her towel and headed to the bedroom, the neighbor loudly made his presence known.

"Neighbor!! Where did you come in from?"

"Well, you remember the day I found you here with your boyfriend cuddling? Now it's my turn!"

He hastily walked toward her. She began screaming at the top of her lungs. He had just grabbed her by the waist when the cop entered. The officer pulled out his pistol.

"Any more movement, and I'm blowing your head off."

The neighbor was confused. He abruptly lifted his hands and placed them at the back of his head. The officer slowly moved toward him and tactfully handcuffed him.

Salma was still in shock. She knelt down and started thanking the officer immensely for his last-minute rescue.

"I promise to give you any amount you want! You have really saved my life."

"Don't worry, lady. You should be thanking Alfonso," the officer replied.

"Alfonso?" She was surprised.

"Yes, your boss. From the look of things, it seems he sensed something bad was going to happen to you."

"Praise be to my boss for his heightened intuition. I will forever be loyal to him," she said, still breathing heavily from the panic. "I've been luckily salvaged."

She got dressed and bought a special supper to celebrate her rescue.

It had been two weeks, and Alfonso had elected his cabinet. He was ready to announce them, so he called a press briefing at State House, where all media stations had availed themselves.

"Good afternoon, everyone. I am delighted to stand here today with the full list of cabinet secretaries who will be assisting me in running my government. I've realized there were many flaws in the last administration—something I intend to correct. That is why I have chosen the most competent individuals, whom I believe will execute their assigned duties effectively.

Before I take more of your time, let me proceed straight to announcing them."

"The Minister for Defense is Abdul Terek, the Minister for Education is Ayhman Jubril..." He continued until he had mentioned all of them. He concluded his speech by congratulating them and inviting them to assist him in building Libya. The appointed individuals would be sworn in once parliament had vetted them.

The following day, Alfonso was in his office when the lawyer, who had a session with him, advised that all the money that had been swindled should be recovered from the MPs' accounts. Alfonso was already making plans to oversee the process.

A total of twenty billion dinars had been recovered. Even though it embittered the involved parties, Alfonso did not care.

The programs he had outlined in his manifesto had already begun running, with every jobless youth receiving their first month's payment. Those who had traveled outside the country were also paid, totaling twelve billion dinars. By that day, all mothers who had recently given birth had received their payments, which amounted to seven billion dinars.

So far, so good—even Salma had witnessed the change in Libya's atmosphere. About a million Libyans had received the monthly reprieve, which was distributed early in the first month, and things had suddenly turned around. Those who had struggled to pay rent had swiftly overcome that hurdle. Those who had struggled to afford food and clothing could now do so without difficulty. Even those living on the brink of poverty were now supported.

It was a beautiful new dawn, and the population was becoming increasingly productive. The people were growing their economic muscle, and Libya was on the path to transformation.

# Chapter| 10

Alfonso held a cabinet meeting, and all the cabinet members were in attendance. They discussed Alfonso's motto: creating a sweet life for everyone. He urged them to embrace it in their service delivery, as it would be their driving force to become the best people to bring development to Libyans. In line with this, he also shared his vision for Africa as a whole and emphasized the sweetness that would be saturated across the continent once there was a common currency for all of Africa.

Everyone was pleased with the idea as they tried to visualize the synchronicity and development in Africa that would be facilitated by such a move. The meeting concluded, and Alfonso returned to his office.

Congressman Steve Curry was planning to visit Libya for a proposed meeting with the Social Affairs Minister of Libya. Plans for the visit were underway. He reported to his senior about the objectives of the meeting, presenting candid facts on the planned terms of agreement to be enacted. His senior approved and gave him the go-ahead.

Two months into Alfonso's tenure, Mr. Steve landed at Tripoli International Airport.

The next day, a government car took him to the office of the Social Affairs Minister. The minister was more than happy to see him, and they greeted each other warmly as the minister welcomed him.

"Hello, sir!"

"Oh, hello, my counterpart... how is the USA?"

"Well, how do I put it? We are the best we've ever been."

"Ah, nice. So, what brings you here?"

"Ah! I am an envoy, as you know, from my government, whose development agenda includes coordinating with emerging countries such as Libya to boost their progress. In essence, this yields mutual benefits as some of my country's investors establish themselves in Libya, thereby remitting money back to the USA."

"That is very well thought out," the Social Affairs Minister said, having been trained in English. "As for us, we are very ready to work together and venture into a long-lasting relationship."

While still in conversation, his secretary suddenly stormed in, excusing herself, citing that the president urgently needed to speak with him. He excused himself and answered the call.

"Hello, yes, boss."

"Oh, you should be in the meeting with the U.S. Secretary of State if I'm not mistaken."

"Yes, sir. I just took some time to answer your call, but we were in the middle of a discussion."

"Okay, I'm sorry for the interruption, but I just wanted you to inform him that the plea they made to the previous government to have their army train on Libyan soil has been granted."

"Okay, definitely, I'll bring it up with him."

"Okay, sir… remember our motto?"

"Conducting sweetness to everybody's life."

"Yes, I see you've got it all figured out for serving your people. As for me, my plan to convene a meeting to formulate an African dollar is underway."

Steve was extraordinarily shocked. That implied that Africa would now be independent and would no longer depend on the USA for its business endeavors. This would be a major blow to the USA, as its dominance in African markets would be reduced, leaving him deeply perturbed.

"Yes, that's my plan."

"Yes, hopefully, it will be successful."

"Okay, continue with your meeting."

The meeting concluded, and the Secretary was driven back to his hotel. He retreated to his room and immediately called the president.

"Boss, there is something critically wrong."

"What is it, Steve? And why do you sound so uneasy?"

"Oh... the president of Libya is planning to establish Africa's central bank, which means Africa will have a common currency, thus breaking free from America's market grip."

The president's tone changed.

"This is costly to us, and it must be stopped at all costs."

"I thought so..." Steve replied.

"Okay, I expect you as soon as possible for a discussion on the matter."

Tony had just received a pardon from the Kiambu governor and was on his way home when he met Mark, the gateman at the bank that Alfonso had robbed.

"Oh... look who's here."

Tony was overwhelmed as the news about Alfonso dawned on him.

"Yes! Alfonso is the president of Libya!"

Tony was ecstatic as he was shown videos of Alfonso's inauguration. He could not believe it. He stopped walking and began dancing in celebration. Instead of heading home first, he decided to visit Kingsley.

"Tony!" Kingsley was bewildered. He ran and hugged him.

Tony became emotional upon seeing his friend's cousin.

"Please do not cry. The worst is behind us."

"Thank you, Kingsley," he said as he wiped his tears.

"Finally, I am free."

"Oh, welcome back! But before we continue... what is this about Alfonso becoming president?"

"Yes, it's true. He is currently the leader of Libya."

"Oh, tell me you're not lying..." Kingsley insisted, unable to believe the news.

Six months had passed, and uprisings had begun forming in Libya. Some rebel groups had started opposing Alfonso's rule.

This weighed heavily on Alfonso, as he was unaware of what had caused the unrest. His wife did all she could to console him, but Alfonso remained troubled.

One Monday afternoon, while Alfonso was cruising the streets of Benghazi, a rebel car suddenly appeared and opened fire in his direction. He had just stepped out to address a crowd. Upon seeing the attack, Alfonso's security team quickly rushed him into the car and sped away. Fortunately, he escaped unharmed.

The following day, a lawyer visited the State House to speak with Alfonso. His wife was sobbing bitterly over what had befallen them. Alfonso excused himself to meet with the lawyer, who introduced himself. Once Alfonso acknowledged him, he proceeded.

"Mr. President, why don't you just fly to another country and give up power?"

Alfonso felt drained. He did not understand why such negativity had emerged.

"I am not willing to abdicate or give up! I shall struggle my way out of this predicament."

"So what will you do?" The lawyer tried to convince him otherwise, but to no avail. Eventually, he left.

Alfonso then called Kingsley, feeling worse than ever.

"Hello, Alfonso, I am so sorry for what you're going through. You have to be strong. Do you know what might have caused this?"

"Oh, cousin, I am just as in the dark as everyone else. I think I'll leave town and go somewhere remote."

"Don't worry, Alfonso."

The next day, the State House correspondent received intelligence that the rebels were planning to camp on the road leading to the State House. Alfonso had to act fast, or he would be compromised.

He decided to relocate to a village in the northwest of Libya. He and his team set out with a convoy of seventy-five cars.

Tony had visited Mark to query the events that led to him being in that position. Mark stared at him and then, all at once, switched.

"Let me tell you... you know what? Alfonso and I go a long way," Mark began. Tony nodded in excitement and anticipation of what he was about to say. "His late dad was a friend of my dad, and that's how I came to know him. Without wasting time, follow me."

So they entered a shrine that was just next to their house.

"Wow!" Tony was amazed.

"You mean to say that..."

"Yes, I am a diviner."

Tony sat in amazement.

Mark performed some incantations and carried out some rituals. In a panic, he disclosed what was happening to Alfonso. (This was the same way he had performed the rituals and discovered that Alfonso was planning to rob a bank, which coincidentally he worked in, making an effort to find him a driver for that cause.)

"Quickly, call anyone close to him," he requested, his voice shaking. So Tony called Kingsley.

"Hello, Kingsley?" Tony said. Mark took the phone.

"Kingsley, something is terribly wrong with Alfonso."

"Yes, he has been experiencing some challenges, but he promised to remain strong."

"It's more serious than you think."

"What are you saying?" Kingsley started tensing.

"As we speak, he is in a caravan escaping... and something terrible is in store for him. I see USA fighter jets coming to wreak havoc on his caravan. They are planning to assassinate him."

"Okay, and how do you know that?"

Tony quickly grabbed the phone and explained, then handed it back to Mark.

"You have to do something. You see, this is the same thing that happened to Muammar Gaddafi—exactly the same."

Without wasting time, Kingsley called the Minister of Defense.

"Hello?" His secretary picked up.

"Hello, can I talk to Suleiman?"

"Sorry, who is this?"

"Oh, this is the president's cousin, and I really need to speak with Suleiman."

"Okay, give me one minute."

"Hello, I heard you wanted to speak to me. Go on."

"There is intelligence information that a USA fighter jet, using NATO satellites, is headed toward Alfonso's convoy in an attempt to strike it with missiles and assassinate the president. Additionally, rebel groups are following them. I need you to assure me that you will do something."

"Oh, thank you for that information," the Minister of Defense was bewildered and immediately contacted the Air Force unit, ordering Alfonso to be traced and sent backup.

The pilot received the information and, with two others, flew to Alfonso's location. Upon arrival, they noticed another plane nearby but had no evidence of its intentions.

Time passed, and the enemy plane launched a missile, hitting Alfonso's fleet. The pilot, confirming their suspicion, carefully aimed and launched a missile at the USA jet, hitting it and causing it to catch fire. The Libyan pilots celebrated their success.

"Long live our president!" the co-pilot exclaimed.

The other pilot added, "Alfonso commands massive respect."

Alfonso witnessed everything that had transpired and was marveled. The damaged car was left behind as they stopped, transferring the driver and one guard to other vehicles. The minister, who was not in the convoy, reassured them and signaled that they were now free to continue their journey.

The journey took five hours, and they arrived in Sirte, Gaddafi's hometown.

They spent a whole week there, occasionally engaging with rebel forces, but Alfonso's forces overpowered them.

"Hey, what will become of our regime?" Alfonso asked Suleiman.

"I am working on a project, and soon, you shall see its fruits. Don't worry. I assure you that everything will be alright."

"Okay, try as much as possible to reinstate my rule."

"On it, sir."

The army accompanying Alfonso spent most of their time protecting him.

One fine morning, Suleiman received intelligence that Abubakar, the leader of the rebel groups, was in El Mina, planning to wreak havoc on Alfonso's rule.

They carefully planned an attack, and the Air Force was assigned the mission.

The pilot flew directly over the building housing the rebels and launched a missile. The rebels inside rushed out with their guns but were no match for the superior weapons. The pilot fired another missile, completely obliterating the militia forces. With a job well executed, the pilot flew back to headquarters.

The phone rang. It was Suleiman.

"Hello, boss?"

"Hello, I've called to inform you that our fighters have executed the leader of the rebel groups."

"Finally! They thought they could tear us down, but now we are back to our original position." Alfonso expressed his relief as tears welled up in his eyes. It was truly uplifting news. He called all those who had accompanied him and assembled them.

"How are you, team? It is my honor to announce that our forces have successfully eliminated Abubakar Mohamed."

Everyone in the crowd broke into shouts of joy. They began giving each other high-fives, and Alfonso joined in the celebration.

"Alfonso! Alfonso! Alfonso!" One of the officials loudly exclaimed fervently, and all others responded cheerfully, "Massive respect!"

Alfonso continued, "We are in the process of pursuing the rebel groups until we destroy them completely."

"Long live Alfonso!" another official shouted, and the crowd responded in unison, "Long live Alfonso!"

The military engaged the groups over the next few days as they perpetrated intense shelling, and they were slowly but surely being defeated.

After five days, the country had once more returned to a peaceful state, and no man could match Alfonso's pride. He was even happier when Tony called him. He could not believe his ears as Tony described how they had intercepted the United States Army, which had intended the worst for him.

The following week, Alfonso was flown back to Tripoli, where he addressed the nation at the State House.

"I greet all of you in the name of our God. I am glad this morning to be addressing you after having regained my powers. Our country has been marked by a sequence of violent events that intended the worst for our beloved nation. It is unfortunate to see individuals who are opposed to our administration. We are saddened by their motives, which were to overthrow me as president, but thanks to our military personnel, that has been averted. I want to call your attention to the way we used to live cohesively and urge that we return to that way of life so that we can restore the love we once had for each other. Together forever," he concluded, just as it was time for the media stations to engage him in some questions.

"Yes," he said, selecting a journalist from Yu TV.

"Thank you, Mr. President. How did the whole experience make you feel, and how did you cope with it?"

> "Well, to be honest, I was quite uncertain, and I didn't know how things would turn out. I really prayed a lot and did some deep introspection. That was the most difficult time in my life. All odds were against me, and I was really scared. A big thanks to our defense minister for bringing things back to normal. I am truly indebted to him. Yes, he is my hero. Next question?"
>
> "Okay, Mr. President, what steps are you going to take to ensure the security of your government and prevent this from happening again?"

Alfonso answered the questions and then ended the briefing. Later, he was scheduled to meet with his cabinet secretaries and was enthusiastic about it. He left and headed to the inner chamber, where he spoke to his assistant and discussed the details of his meeting, which was scheduled for around two o'clock.

"Hey dear, that was a nice speech you gave," she said.

"Come here," he replied as he hugged her and led her to the dining room.

"Oh, honey, that was the worst crisis we have ever faced."

"That's right, honey. Remember when we were in the convoy headed to Sirte?"

Immediately, Alfonso became emotional and lay on Amina's chest.

"I will always be there for you, hun."

"And I promise to serve my people with all my heart and to give them my best."

"Hey, do you still hold onto the idea of the African Central Bank?"

"Honestly, with all these happenings…"

Aisha placed a finger on his lips.

"I know exactly how you feel, but first, let us meet with the staff who used to work for Muammar, okay? I'm sure they will help guide you in achieving your agenda. ALFONSO IS LOGICALLY EQUIVALENT TO MASSIVE RESPECT."

He held her hand as he shed a tear.

Lunch was served, and they enjoyed it while Alfonso made some quick follow-ups on some developments that the ministries were handling.

Yes, the projects had stalled because of the chaos, but now they could resume where they had left off. He directed the involved ministers to take action.

That was actually what he had planned to discuss with them—developments.

Alfonso spent some time catching up on the ongoing news, as the stations were critically analyzing the trajectory of the chaos. The steps taken in the near future would certainly determine the fate of their nation. Alfonso became even more attentive, knowing he had a significant role to play in reinstating the country's previous economic progress.

"Time has come," the State House attendant alerted Alfonso. He stood up, adjusted his collar, straightened his belt, and started walking out of the TV room. He went directly to the limousine as his aide saluted him. It was a forty-five-minutes-drive to Al-nakhlatein town hall, where cabinet secretaries had convened.

Immediately upon entering the conference room, the ministers began clapping as Alfonso greeted them and first thanked them for standing by him during the tribulations. He expressed his deepest gratitude to those who accompanied him to Sirte during the close call when a missile hit their convoy. Jokingly, he said it was the most distinguished fleet, consisting of seventy-five cars, making everyone laugh.

"Before I continue, I would like to call the CS for Defense to the front to share how he managed such a crucial moment and the life-saving decisions he took."

Everybody clapped as Suleiman marched to the front.

"Good morning, ladies and gentlemen."

"Good morning, sir."

"Well, I deeply appreciate all of you because, in one way or another, you played a part in bringing us to where we are today. Special regards to my boss, Mr. Alfonso, who was very instrumental in helping us overcome the crisis. Without his competent wisdom and insight, we would not have managed to defeat the USA attacks and neutralize the rebel groups. He constantly checked up on me and offered a shoulder to lean on whenever I felt overwhelmed. It is heartbreaking to imagine that the United States wanted our dearest president dead, but we will not be deterred—not now, not ever. Stronger together!" he shouted as he raised his right hand.

"Stronger together!" everyone exclaimed.

"Okay, that is all I have to say. May all of you enjoy the fruits of Alfonso's style of leadership. Thank you." He concluded and returned to his seat as everyone clapped. Alfonso, who had been seated, stood up, joined in the applause, and cleared his throat.

"Thank you so much, Mr. Suleiman. I hope Allah blesses you beyond expectation for the great work you have done."

"The main reason I called you here is to deliberate on development issues. We are all aware that most of our ministries had begun laying the groundwork for various development activities. I implore everyone to get back to business. Let us remember why we are in these positions—to serve Libyans, which should be our top priority.

For the ministries that are yet to initiate projects, pull up your socks and start as soon as possible.

I had initially wanted to establish an African Central Bank, which would ultimately lead to a common African currency. This would allow us to utilize and benefit from our resources to the fullest. This initiative had the potential to free Africa from the shackles of poverty and unproductivity. However, I recently learned that the attempted assassination by the United States had everything to do with this. I am deeply disappointed, but my wife is working on some interventions.

With that, I will conclude and release you, as I have some pressing work to attend to at the office."

Alfonso exited the room as all the CSs clapped. The meeting lasted about an hour as they had other issues of discussion and then he headed back to his office.

Within a short time, he was already at his annex, scheduled to meet with some law enforcers from the previous government.

His office affairs manager had prepared him, and he was ready.

The first guest was a former defense minister. Their initial interaction made it clear that what had happened to Alfonso was unlikely to have occurred during the previous regime. Alfonso was amazed, as the minister explained that the reason for his visit was to help Alfonso close the loopholes in his government once and for all.

This was one piece of advice Alfonso took to heart. He ordered investigations to determine which political leaders from his party had participated in the uprising as the inquiries were underway.

That day, he met with his deputy, Mr. Omar, who had just woken up from a coma amidst all the ongoing events.

Alfonso, along with some other government officials, streamed into the national hospital and was delighted to see him. Omar was also happy, even more so now that the unrest had ended and Alfonso was back in power. Alfonso engaged him in conversation, and they both expressed their happiness.

The two spent some time together as Alfonso assured Omar that everything would be alright.

Alfonso returned home, feeling glad because things were going just as expected.

At home, he found that the cook had arrived. "Hi..."

"Hello! You definitely made it through Gaddafi's tenure fifteen years ago."

"Yes, my president, it's my pleasure to come back to the statehouse."

"I really want to house you for the next few days. Is that okay with you?"

"I'm perfectly fine with that."

"Okay, go ahead, settle in, and feel at home. Then we will discuss more. Is that alright?"

"Alright, sir. First and foremost, thank you for inviting me over. I am more than ready to assist where necessary."

"Splendid."

"Alfonso, tell me, what do you love most about me?"

Amina inquired with awe. Alfonso blushed at her heightened care.

"Oh, honey, you make me feel special whenever I'm around you, and you surround me with immense warmth." They hugged as they savored the moment.

"I'm so glad that you managed to bring the cook."

"Yes, dear... We'll harness the wisdom of our hero. Don't you think so?"

"Exactly! And that's why I love you, dear."

"Oh." She kissed him fervently.

"Honey, this is the most sentimental moment since we met."

"I agree, hun."

"I actually feel so lucky since my government is already falling back into place."

"Yes, dear. That was just a passing cloud, and now you can continue with your grand agenda."

"Mmm, baby."

"Yes, baby. Africa has lagged behind in so many areas, and creating the African Central Bank will really go a long way in placing Africa where it's supposed to be economically."

"Honey, you are definitely going to achieve that."

"The minerals, which are abundantly available in Africa, will be sold at a higher price, and there will be flexibility among the countries. How sweet is that?"

"Honestly, dear, you are advocating for a good cause, and you don't fully comprehend the lives you will impact."

"That's so marvelous. So how are you planning to go about it?"

"Probably by coordinating with my South African counterpart, Anthony Sanzille, and engaging him in the same, since he is in a more advantageous economic position. If I get his consent, I will have made good progress. You see, if I manage to convince them of the benefits, then I am halfway there. With his influence, he can convince other African leaders, and there we go. Then, we just need like-minded individuals, which will guarantee the success of my vision. But I can actually frame it as not being easy."

"That is a guarantee. You have a lot on your plate."

"Oh, honey, I don't care as long as Africa unites."

"Together we stand, divided we fall," Amina responded enthusiastically.

"Okay, honey, it's time for dinner. Will you join me?"

"Why not?"

They left for the dining room and found that Amina's favorite delicacy had been prepared, which Alfonso had also grown to love. They enjoyed the meal as they bonded and later retired to bed.

It was the weekend, and Alfonso was spending it meeting his relatives and some of his officials. He woke up at nine on Saturday morning and headed to the gym. After exercising for an hour, he showered and met his wife, who kissed him good morning as they chatted about whom to spend their weekend with. Amina hinted at spending it with her family and younger brother, whom she had really missed.

"Well, I had already made prior arrangements with them, so it's just a matter of having them ferried here, and then we can have some quality time together."

"Yeah, that's a good idea."

Within two hours, Amina's mom, dad, and younger brother had arrived, brought by the driver. (The youngest brother had visited their aunt.) They were led to the statehouse, and as soon as Amina saw them, she ran to greet them, overjoyed.

"Alfonso!" They enthusiastically hugged him.

"You are so lucky!"

Alfonso laughed. "Welcome to my official residence."

"Wow, the place is beautiful."

"Yes! Oh, hi, Junior?" Amina hugged her younger brother.

"Sister, will I become like Uncle one day?" her little brother asked innocently, as they all saw his ambition.

His father bent down. "Junior, if you want to become like your uncle, you have to study hard, pass your examinations, and then pursue a degree. Is that okay?"

He nodded as the others shared in the joyful moment.

"Oh, you surely have an ambitious kid," Alfonso noted as they all laughed.

"Welcome in."

They went to the guest room and talked about the peaceful time after the sad episode. Amina's parents expressed how concerned they had been and how much they had prayed for him. Alfonso admitted that it was the most disheartening moment of his life. He had not seen a possibility of making it through, but things had gotten better.

"Yes, it was a very desperate time."

"I hear there were some attacks on your convoy."

Alfonso paused for a moment, taking a deep breath. "Sadly, the United States government was trying to play cards with me."

"The US government?" Both parents seemed shocked as Alfonso reiterated his statement.

"Why would they do that?"

"Only they know better."

"That is absurd! So how did you manage to handle it?"

"The defense minister was alert and acted accordingly."

"We are sure that you had a limited chance of surviving the disjunction."

"That's true, especially since the rebel groups had followed me to Sirte. It was an effort to eliminate me. I'm telling you, it was only through the help of God that I'm alive today."

Alfonso spent the rest of the day with them, and when they left, they thanked him for the good time they had shared. Amina also spent some time playing with her little brother and promised to reward him if he passed his end-term exam, which he promised to do. He admitted that he envied Alfonso and had found motivation to work hard and succeed.

That Sunday, Alfonso woke up early and attended Union Church in Tripoli. After addressing the congregation, he returned to the statehouse, where Malcolm had already arrived. Alfonso was overjoyed to see him. He jumped up and quickly went to greet him. Their mood was elated as they had not seen each other for quite a long time.

"Alfonso, you know I'm very proud of you."

"Yes, actually, I'm even prouder."

"The best uncle has never forsaken me, from our somber days to these magnificent ones."

They gave each other a fist bump. Malcolm retrieved a photo he had taken at the supermarket.

"Check this... Bali."

To Mr. Hassan: "You mean Hassan, the opposition leader?"

"Take your time... go through the whole note. I know that we had plans to kill the maniac on the day Abdul and I killed his family in Kenya, but we never succeeded... and he escaped. Now we just have to wait and see what will transpire over the course of these five years. Just try to bear it."

Alfonso gasped for air as he flashed back to memories of his loving daddy, his mommy, and his dearest sister. He held his head in his hands as tears began to trickle down his face.

"Uncle, that former trade minister was responsible for my greatest pain?!"

"Yes, there you have the full evidence."

His voice cracked. "Then I am going to give him the most brutal revenge, I swear..."

"Yes, Alfonso, and I will be your accomplice, just as I promised you. Finally, Alfonso, we will have our revenge... finally!"

Alfonso went to sleep, struggling to comprehend that his rival had begun opposing him so early. Because of his destiny, he had to lose his family... how unfortunate. But first, Alfonso recollected himself so as not to be completely affected by the news, since it would have disrupted his ability to function, which would be disastrous.

Later that day, the cook came over to Alfonso while he was watching TV and greeted him.

"Hi, boss, you seem stressed. Is anything the matter?"

"Oh, Junet, thanks for your concern. Everything is okay, just the normal daily stressors we encounter..."

"And you? How about you? Is everything alright?"

"Yes, sir, I was just reminiscing about my days working for the former president..."

"Yes... so tell me, what is your greatest memory?"

"Oh, my greatest one is when His Excellency came to me one day and broke the news that he had acquired a property for me in Sabha at a cost of two hundred and fifty thousand dinars. I couldn't believe my ears! He gave me a two-week break to go and move my family. When I went, my family could not believe it.

We actually moved from a bedsitter to a three-bedroom bungalow with two floors. It was the best gift I could ever receive... Also, you had expressed that you wanted to take notes from his term?"

"Yes, Junet."

"So, are you ready to go out of your way to make the State House staff content and happy working for you? Because His Excellency Gaddafi was really cautious with every one of the staff in the State House."

"Okay," Alfonso listened.

"I remember one day, his driver's parents were sick... imagine, he traveled all the way to Murzuq."

Alfonso seemed captivated by the story.

"You mean he went to the driver's home?"

He felt challenged as he saw the need to be more intentional in handling his staff. By the end of the discussion, he was deeply moved. Even though Gaddafi's tenure was marked by myriad challenges, it was also one of the best regimes in terms of service delivery. People accredited this to his residential peace, considering that only under a peaceful environment can one thrive to such levels of success.

Later that evening, Amina returned from an event she had attended as the First Lady, brought home by the drivers.

She came back overjoyed, eager to share a story with Alfonso.

"Honey, I was giving a speech at a gathering when a lady stood up from among the congregants and wanted to speak. So I gave her a chance and she said she is the mother to your secretary. That very day, she survived an attempted rape because the officer arrived just in time. She was very grateful for your intervention and wished you all the very best."

Alfonso, feeling rejuvenated, smiled. "You are actually my success mate."

He tickled her as they both enjoyed the moment.

"And as for me," Alfonso sighted, "I finally got a chance to meet Junet. Honey, Gaddafi was really a great guy! He actually bought a three-bedroom bungalow for him."

Amina's face brightened up. "That was so kind of him... what?! We have a lot to do if we want to emulate him... that's certain."

# Chapter | 11

Alfonso had ordered a call to be made to his South African counterpart, and he went to a special room dedicated to Zoom and other important meetings.

"Many greetings, Mr. Antony."

"Greetings to you, sir. It has come to my attention the immense disadvantage that our continent is enduring due to the instability of our currencies," Alfonso said.

Mr. Antony Sanzille, the South African president, seemed puzzled. "I don't get you, sir. Can you elaborate further?"

"There is a notion that we could achieve much more development if we formed an African Central Bank..."

Immediately, Antony's face shone with brilliance. It was like an epiphany. "You are the greatest mind I've ever come across, sir. That was the ideology of the late Muammar Gaddafi, and I can attest from his development track record that there was much he had visualized for Africa. Actually, the idea is even more relevant now since it will curb many issues, such as exploitation from the West, corruption in Africa, and economic inflexibility, ultimately leading to significant economic growth."

"You are right. So how do we proceed from here?"

"Why don't we schedule a meeting on this matter?" Alfonso suggested.

"Oh, that would really be appropriate. When exactly?"

"In two weeks' time. Is that okay?"

"Yes, it's okay with me."

He ended the call and went back to the office, then ordered a call to be made to Omar. Upon answering, Omar was excited to hear that his idea about uniting Africa had gained some traction.

Alfonso informed him, and Omar expressed great joy about the whole project.

"Yes, so I'll be flying to South Africa for about three days exactly two weeks from now. I hope you will run the country on my behalf."

"No problem, sir. I am up to the task."

Alfonso was scheduled to meet with his defense minister in the morning and his finance minister in the evening.

He waited for about thirty minutes, and then his defense minister arrived.

"Hi, Mr. Suleiman."

"Hi too, my president. I hope you had a good weekend."

"Yes, I had a relaxing time and got to run some of my errands. So, let's get down to business, shall we?"

"Of course, sir."

"It has come to my attention that some MPs in government, including those from my party, have been colluding with rebel groups. Are you aware of that?"

"Sadly, I am aware, and that should be the last thing expected from a member claiming to demonstrate allegiance to his political party."

"So I want you to hunt them down and forward their names as soon as possible. Is that clear?"

"Yes, it's clear, boss."

They discussed other agendas Alfonso had, which took two hours. When lunchtime arrived, Alfonso went to the dining room to have his meal.

Within an hour, he was done and went back to the office. His finance minister was already waiting. Once Alfonso arrived, the minister knocked on the door and was allowed in.

"Good afternoon, Mr. Zechariah."

"Good afternoon, sir. I hope you've been well."

"Exactly, sir. So, I've called you here regarding the African Central Bank."

"Oh, the project you've been working on?"

"Yes."

"Oh yes, what about it?"

"Imagine, it's making noteworthy progress."

Zechariah was excited. "You mean its course is underway?"

"Exactly, sir. And that's now your responsibility. I want you to develop relevant modules capturing the capital remittance of each member country, the mode of tax collection, and a module that allows for the appropriate allocation of resources to each member state."

"Oh... that is quite a challenge, but I accept. Entrusting me with such a project only demonstrates the extent of your trust in me, and I promise to deliver the best. You can count on me."

"Well, I'll take your word for it. You have one month to achieve that."

"Ah, a month is quite enough time."

Two weeks passed, and the appointed time for the visit to South Africa had arrived. That morning, Alfonso packed his bags with the new clothing that the State House's presidential affairs office had bought for him. They first held a prayer session, led by a pastor from the church Alfonso attended. Then, Alfonso set out on his journey. He bid farewell to his wife, hugging her tightly, and she promised to pray for him throughout the trip.

They entered a limousine headed to Tripoli International Airport. Alfonso had prepared a PowerPoint document on the matters of discussion and had it saved in his email. The flight took 20 hours, and they landed at Johannesburg International Airport, where Alfonso was welcomed by some envoys of the national government.

"Alfonso is logically equivalent to massive respect!" one of the envoys remarked as he bowed. The convoy then headed to the State House in Pretoria.

As they arrived at the facade, Mr. Antony came out, visibly delighted. "How are you, my dear friend?" he asked.

He was perplexed beyond words to meet Alfonso. Alfonso approached him and hugged him as the officer assigned to him saluted, leaving the two in a jovial mood.

"Welcome!"

"You sure are a South African king."

"But nowadays, enforcing laws and ensuring everyone follows them is the new system of kingship," Antony joked.

He was warmly welcomed as one of the officers took his belongings and walked behind them hastily. They proceeded to the living room, where Alfonso was served a cold juice. That day was spent with Antony giving Alfonso a brief history of South Africa as he acclimatized to the environment.

The following day arrived, and they were back to business. They discussed the whole idea and devised ways to persuade other African leaders to join the initiative.

After six months, almost every African country, apart from Libya and Eswatini, had accepted the proposal. For the latter, it was understandable since it was a monarchy. King Ebuka's son was on his deathbed, suffering from a serious illness. The king witnessed his son's final moments and heard his last wish: that his father would join in the merging of African countries. After his son's burial, King Ebuka contacted his South African counterpart and expressed his desire to join the alliance. It was also an uphill task to convince the royal family of Libya, but after a long struggle, they eventually agreed.

The date for the official coronation of the United States of Africa had been set, and Antony Sanzille was unanimously voted in as the president of the union.

The coronation was held in South Africa, attended by all former heads of state. It was a colorful event, with dignitaries from all over the world—except America—in attendance. The ceremony began with a prayer and was followed by the United States of Africa anthem, which had been formulated by a selected commission.

It was then followed by a showcase of the union's rich culture through songs and dances... as Alfonso's story was highlighted—the journey he undertook not only in fighting for that moment but also in shaping the face and future of Africa. His deputy, who was sitting next to him, sought to praise Alfonso, but he shed some tears at the acrimony of what was transpiring—on account of what he had to endure and go through just to achieve that feat. He was as humbled as ever with every single line that was being read at Alexandra Stadium.

"And I will not leave out this fact—Alfonso is logically equivalent to massive respect..." Everyone cheered as the president of South Africa was called to the front to take his oath.

The newly appointed head of the Supreme Court of Africa stood at the podium to administer the oath.

"Mr. Anthony, repeat after me," she recited.

"I, Anthony Sanzile, do accept the position of the President of the United States of Africa, as elected, and I promise to diligently conduct my duties with utmost sincerity and uphold the constitution of the union..." (The states had already formulated a constitution by compiling the commonalities of African constitutions and arriving at one distinct document.) "...and I promise to uphold the law and serve with all my heart. So help me, God."

As he finished, the crowd erupted into applause, cheering him on for the great achievement.

That moment marked the realization of Muammar Gaddafi's vision—or should I say, it was Gaddafi's unmisplaced glory.

Oh, what a great moment of favor for Africa and its member states!

At that time, the African dollar was stronger than the US dollar—one African dollar was equivalent to ten US dollars.

The world's major powers, including Europe and China, entered into deals with the President of the United States of Africa. It was a double profit, as the price of African minerals had increased five hundred times their initial value—a major victory for the United States of Africa.

The profits were so immense that Anthony used part of them to initiate development projects in every single state. The countries whose development had stalled due to corruption and poor governance received the largest share of the funds. Children gained access to quality healthcare, social amenities were established, and more hospitals were built. The most remarkable development was that people began moving to more advanced countries, securing new livelihoods, and starting businesses. Oh, it was the realization of the sweetest life—a life that had never been conceptualized by man or any African spirit.

Alfonso had returned home and spent his days reconnecting with people with whom he had long formed close bonds. He was entitled to government privileges, but not as before, where he had an aide-de-camp and traveled in government convoys. He received a monthly salary and allowances and had security at his home. For Amina, this was the greatest decision Alfonso had ever made, and what delighted him most was knowing that his name would be remembered in history.

A few months after the coalition government was formed, Malcolm went to the same supermarket where he usually shopped. As he walked down the aisle, he noticed something peculiar—the man he had met last time was heading to the cashier. Suddenly, a sensation ran down his spine. He couldn't fully grasp how to react, but he was in for the thrill. He immediately looked for a bodaboda rider and instructed him to follow the man wherever he went.

The man exited the supermarket and boarded a bodaboda. Malcolm and the rider followed at a distance. About two kilometers from the shopping center, the man stopped and entered a black gate. That was when Malcolm excitedly called Alfonso, who was overly eager to undertake a revenge mission. Alfonso urged Malcolm to take his time studying the terrain and gathering information about the perpetrators.

Malcolm first headed home to develop a more structured plan for the attack. He needed to determine how many men lived in that house, what weapons they possessed, and who else had been involved in the killing of Alfonso's family. How had they known Alfonso was set to occupy the next leadership seat? He met with Alfonso to discuss their findings. Alfonso, deeply intent on avenging his family's death, came up with an idea—he asked Malcolm to get the man's name from the neighbors.

After a day of active investigation, Malcolm finally obtained the man's full name. Alfonso ran his profile through intelligence, and to his alarm, the findings were shocking. A friend working in intelligence had helped him retrieve the information.

The records revealed that the man was involved in the dark world, with shrines in Sabha. At one point, he and another man named Tawakal—who had been living with him—had traveled to Kenya, where they executed an entire family. The two men were also affiliated with Hassan, the former opposition leader who had lost to Alfonso in the previous elections held in Libya.

They later confirmed that the two men were living together.

Malcolm had taken some time at the location of the two goons and was coincidentally approached by one of them, who wanted to know the time. "Young man, have you ever gone to Kenya?"

"What!!!" The guy was shocked. "Do you know me?"

"I don't know you, but I am a diviner, and I can trace something strange in your life."

"So will you choose to follow me, or do you..." Even before he finished, he alluded to following him as they boarded a matatu. He sent a message to Alfonso to show up at his home for the final revenge activity. He denoted that he had convinced one of them to come to his home, hoping that the other would join him.

"Don't forget to carry the appropriate tools, as I have a few at my home. So don't you think it's appropriate to call your other counterpart?"

"Who?" He was overly shocked.

"Oh, the one you traveled to Kenya with? Yes, it's a mates' affair."

"Okay, let me see if I'll reach him."

And so he engaged with him, and after telling him he was not occupied, he explained what had happened and that he was expecting him at the Benghazi hillside center at the house he would show him.

"What!! You mean our previous encounters were not fully cleared?" The guy wondered.

"If the claims of this man were anything to go by..."

"I'll be there in twenty minutes."

So they arrived at Malcolm's house, and within a couple of minutes, the other fellow arrived.

"So, guys, do you want to know why you are here?"

"Oh, don't be sarcastic. You told us to come here so that you can demystify some facet of our lives, right?" they responded.

"Well, there is a better person well-suited for that."

Alfonso who had passed through the back door showed up.

Suddenly, the men recognized him.

"You've got to be kidding!" one of the men exclaimed.

They held each other cognizant of their fate.

"Now what will I do?" the other panicked as tears began trickling down their cheeks and Alfonso loved every bit of it.

"Well, you guys made sure my whole family was dead. You brutally murdered my dad and my mom, and you didn't even spare my sister. Well, open your mouth," he frantically instructed the first man while he begged for mercy. Malcom was keeping guard with the pistol in case of any silly move.

He instructed Malcolm to bring the instruments as he removed his pistol to ensure no one moved.

Within no time, he had come with the finger guillotine, a burning jiko, and a bottle full of acid.

"Well, you guys made sure my whole family was dead. You brutally murdered my dad and my mom, and you didn't even spare my sister. Well, open your mouth," he frantically instructed the first man while he begged for mercy. Malcom was keeping guard with the pistol in case of any silly move.

Malcolm pointed the gun at the first one, leaving him no option but to comply. Alfonso inserted the burning coal into his mouth. He shouted helplessly and was instructed to swallow them. He let out a loud scream of pain as the other sweated profusely, panicking and shaking like a leaf.

His turn came. Alfonso took the finger guillotine and slit his fingers one by one as Tawakal let out screams of excruciating pain. He cried helplessly as blood oozed from the slit fingers.

"Hey, looks like the man on the floor is passing out from the pain. Let's take him to the incinerator."

So they carried him and—schunk!—threw his body in. The man could not bear the pain and tried to get out, but Alfonso and Malcolm were smart enough to tie both of his hands from the back.

He cried in anguish as his body was left to burn in the fiery furnace.

They went to the second one, finished cutting his fingers, and did the same. Again, they took him to the incinerator and threw his body in.

That's when Alfonso called Tony, who was overly excited.

"Man, I am so happy after finding out the whole truth."

"Oh, so there was a twist to it…"

"Wait, Tony! The former Libyan trade minister had connived against me, and imagine—they had consulted the spiritual world and understood that I'd pose a potential threat."

"Okay, that makes sense now."

"Truly, a negative and a positive attract. If it were not for my keen stand and your cooperation, you would not have made it to the great person that you are today. And you know what? Alfonso is logically equivalent to massive respect."

Tony alerted him that he was flying to Libya in the next two days, and both chuckled at how callous the revenge had been.

Alfonso gave Malcolm a fist bump as he hugged him fervently.

"I told you we would have our revenge," he said, delighted that he had fulfilled his promise.

"Thank you, Uncle. They might have taken Mommy and Daddy, but they didn't take you! Thank you," he hugged him once more.

That same week, Alfonso saw on the news that Hassan had contracted a deadly skin disease, causing his skin to rot, and he had died. It was a double victory as Malcolm called Alfonso, and they celebrated.

Two days later, Tony arrived. He was welcomed by Alfonso at Tripoli International Airport with Aisha, Moses, and Amina. They carried his bags as Alfonso was overexcited to meet his old-time friend.

They went to Alfonso's house, and Tony was fascinated by the whole story of how Aisha had led to Alfonso's rise to such great extents.

"Hey Tony, tomorrow shall I take you to the former Libyan statehouse?"

Tony could not believe that his efforts had such humongous results.

"Alfonso, I am proud of you, and you'll always be in my heart and my life."

"And I am grateful for everything you have done for me, even the little sacrifices."

"Oh, to God be the glory," Tony answered, and the two hugged each other.

"Friends for life," Alfonso declared.

"Friends for life," Tony reiterated.

Aisha was cooking dinner for them after the two had visited the statehouse. Tony was truly perplexed. He could not imagine that his friend was enjoying all that luxury by himself, with security detail added to it.

Tony stayed for one week and then returned home.

Alfonso agreed that, with the help of Kingsley, he would assist Mark in visiting him to show gratitude for what he had done for him.

He consulted Kingsley, who was glad that Mark felt recognized.

Finally, two of Alfonso's relatives—the mother of Kingsley and his cousin, who had comforted him during his family's burial—were also in the group, together with Kingsley and Mark.

They landed at Tripoli International Airport, and Alfonso and his team were there to pick them up. They were immensely excited, with Mark taking a picture with Alfonso and sending it to his family.

Alfonso was really grateful to Mark, as he came to understand that some people in life are sent with earnestness to liberate others.

They reached home, and the family lived happily ever after.

9 789348 892188

Printed at Repro India Ltd.